More Homemaking Blueprints

More Homemaking Blueprints

Diane B. Orton
Renee B. Malouf

Illustrated by Annette Ward

Bookcraft
Salt Lake City, Utah

Library of Congress Catalog Card Number: 97-74881

ISBN 1-57008-333-9

2nd Printing, 1998

Printed in the United States of America

Contents

Introduction

We appreciate the kind comments we have received on the first volume of *Homemaking Blueprints.* In this volume we have included luncheon ideas, family recipes, and craft instructions. To help meet Relief Society goals, we have also incorporated literacy and service miniclasses into the plans for homemaking meetings. We hope you will carefully evaluate what opportunities for service to others are available in your area.

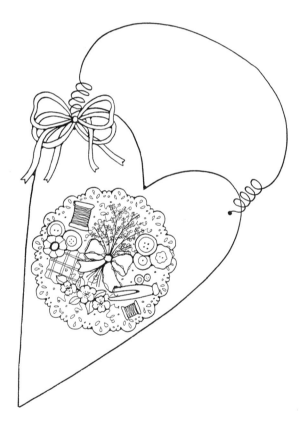

Homemaking Day Luncheons

The general Relief Society has encouraged the sisters to serve a light luncheon or dinner at homemaking meeting. The cost of these meals is to be included in the homemaking day budget (see Relief Society Handbook, p. 35). In addition to providing an opportunity for the sisters to socialize in a relaxed atmosphere, the homemaking meal can be a means to encourage the sisters to cook nutritious meals for their families.

We have included large-quantity recipes for your use. Also included is a blank recipe form which you could photocopy and then use to write down the recipes served at the luncheon. The recipes may then be photocopied and distributed to those attending the homemaking meeting. Encourage the sisters to cook for their families!

Chicken Enchiladas

6 1/2 cups water
1 small onion, diced
1 teaspoon salt

2 stalks celery, diced
8 skinless chicken breasts

Wash chicken breasts; add water, onion, celery, and salt. Bring to a boil over high heat. Reduce heat to medium and cook until chicken is thoroughly done—approximately 30 minutes.

Filling and Sauce

6 cups Monterey Jack cheese, grated
6 cups medium-sharp cheddar cheese, grated
6 10 1/2-ounce cans condensed cream of chicken soup
3 10 1/2-ounce cans condensed cream of mushroom soup
3 16-ounce cartons sour cream

3 4-ounce cans diced green chiles
2 onions, diced
1/2 cup salsa
3 dozen flour tortillas
3 cans sliced olives (2 1/4 oz.)
Dried chives
3 cups medium-sharp cheddar cheese, grated

Chicken Enchiladas
Filling and Sauce (cont.)

Mix together well all the ingredients except the tortillas, olives, chives, and 3 cups cheddar cheese. Stir in 1 cup of reserved chicken broth.

Cut cooled chicken breasts into small cubes. Spoon a heaping tablespoon of cubed chicken along the center of a flour tortilla. Over the top of the chicken, spread a large tablespoon of the sauce mixture. Roll tortilla and place in 9x13-inch casserole dish. Repeat with remaining tortillas. After tortillas are all rolled and placed in casserole dishes, thin the remaining sauce with reserved chicken broth (leave onions and celery in broth). It may not require all of the reserved broth, but you will need enough sauce to pour over all tortillas. Sprinkle cheese over top of casserole. Sprinkle sliced olives and dried chives over top of cheese. Cover casseroles with plastic wrap and store in refrigerator overnight (tortillas are much better if allowed to stand overnight before cooking). Bake at 350 degrees for 30 minutes, uncovered. **(36 servings)**

Pita Pockets

3 pounds ground beef
$1^1/2$ cups chopped onion
1 cup chopped green pepper
$1/3$ cup Worcestershire sauce
$1/3$ cup soy sauce
2 tablespoons garlic powder

1 tablespoon ground cumin
2 teaspoons Italian seasoning
18 pita breads, cut in half
6 tomatoes, diced
9 cups shredded lettuce

In a skillet, brown beef, onion, and green pepper; drain. Add Worcestershire sauce, soy sauce, garlic powder, cumin, and Italian seasoning. Mix well. Simmer for 10 minutes. Spoon meat mixture into halved pita breads, spoon on sauce (recipe below), and top with tomatoes and lettuce.

Sauce

$1^1/2$ cups soy sauce
$3/4$ cup red wine vinegar
$1/3$ cup Worcestershire sauce

$1^1/2$ teaspoons onion powder
$1^1/2$ teaspoons garlic powder
$1^1/2$ teaspoons Italian seasoning

Combine ingredients in a saucepan and bring to a boil. Simmer for 5 minutes.

(36 servings)

Mexican Lasagna

9 pounds ground beef
$1^1/2$ cups chopped onion
9 envelopes taco seasoning mix
3 15-ounce cans tomato sauce
3 $14^1/2$-ounce cans diced tomatoes (with liquid)

20 10-inch flour tortillas, cut into 2-inch strips
2 cups salsa
3 pounds medium-sharp cheddar cheese, shredded

In large skillets, brown beef and onion. Drain. Add taco seasoning, tomato sauce, and tomatoes with liquid. Reduce heat and simmer for 10 minutes. Spoon about 2 cups of beef mixture into each of three 9x13x2-inch casserole dishes. Top with a single layer of tortilla strips. Drizzle 3 or 4 tablespoons of salsa over tortilla strips. Sprinkle cheese over salsa. Repeat layers twice more in each casserole dish. Cover with foil and bake at 350 degrees for 40 minutes or until bubbly. Remove foil and sprinkle with remaining shredded cheese. Return to oven until cheese is melted. **(36 servings)**

Chicken-Ham Casserole

9 cups cubed cooked
 chicken
7 cups cubed cooked ham
2 quarts (8 cups) thick
 homemade white sauce
 (see recipe in the
 February section)
4 cups chicken broth

4 cups grated Parmesan
 cheese
1 12-ounce can sliced
 mushrooms, undrained
2 1/2 pounds frozen peas
1 pound spaghetti, broken
 into 2-inch lengths,
 cooked, and drained

Combine all ingredients; mix well. Spoon into 3 or 4 9x13x2-inch casserole dishes. Cover with foil and bake at 350 degrees for 1 hour. **(24 servings)**

Chicken Salad

10 cups diced cooked chicken
8 cups cooked mini-shell
 macaroni
8 cups diced celery
3 cups seedless green or red
 grape halves (measure
 after halved)

20 hard-boiled eggs, diced
2 20-ounce cans pineapple
 tidbits, drained

Combine above ingredients and stir together. Pour sauce (recipe below) over salad and toss to coat. Chill for at least 1 hour before serving.

Sauce

1 quart mayonnaise
2 cups sour cream
2 cups whipped topping
1/3 cup lemon juice

1/2 cup sugar
1 teaspoon salt
2 cups cashews, chopped

Stir ingredients together until smooth. If desired, may reserve cashews and fold in just before serving. **(50 servings)**

Coleslaw

12 pounds cabbage, finely shredded
10 medium green peppers, cut into very thin slices
3 cups red wine vinegar
3 cups sugar

2 tablespoons salt
2 teaspoons pepper
2 teaspoons paprika
$1^1/2$ cups mayonnaise
$1^1/2$ cups salad dressing

After cabbage and peppers have been prepared, place in separate bowls, cover, and chill until ready to assemble salad. About 45 minutes before serving, combine vinegar, sugar, salt, pepper, and paprika. Pour over cabbage and let set for 30 minutes. Drain well. Add green peppers, mayonnaise, and salad dressing to cabbage. Toss together. **(50 servings)**

Creamy Orange Salad

3 20-ounce cans crushed pineapple, undrained
3 6-ounce packages orange-flavored gelatin
6 cups buttermilk

3 8-ounce cartons whipped topping, thawed
$1^1/2$ cups finely chopped pecans

In a saucepan, bring pineapple with juice to a boil. Remove from heat and add gelatin. Stir to dissolve. Add buttermilk and mix well. Cool to room temperature. Fold pineapple mixture and pecans into whipped topping. Pour into three 9x13x2-inch casserole dishes. Refrigerate overnight. **(36 servings)**

Vanilla Fruit Salad

3 20-ounce cans pineapple
chunks, undrained
1/3 cup lemon juice
2 5.9-ounce packages instant
vanilla pudding mix

4 15-ounce cans mandarin
oranges, drained
5 apples, chopped
1 1/2 cups pecans, chopped

Drain pineapple and reserve juice. Add lemon juice to pineapple juice; then add enough water to make 3 cups of liquid. Place pudding mix in large bowl and stir in pineapple juice until thickened (4–6 minutes). Fold in pineapple chunks, oranges, apples, and pecans. Pour into two 9x13x2-inch casserole dishes. Chill overnight. **(30 servings)**

Fruit Cocktail Bars

1 1/2 cups sugar
2 eggs
1 17-ounce can fruit cocktail,
undrained
2 teaspoons vanilla

2 1/4 cups flour
1 1/2 teaspoons baking soda
1 teaspoon salt
1 1/2 cups flaked coconut
1 cup chopped pecans

Cream sugar and eggs. Add fruit cocktail and vanilla; mix well. Combine flour, baking soda, and salt; add to creamed mixture and mix together. Pour into a greased and floured 10x15x1-inch baking pan. Sprinkle with coconut and pecans. Bake at 350 degrees for 25 minutes or until cake tests done. Drizzle glaze (recipe below) over hot cake. Cool and cut into bars.

Glaze

1/2 cup sugar
1/4 cup butter or margarine
1 tablespoon milk

1 tablespoon lemon juice
1 teaspoon vanilla

Combine sugar, butter, milk, and lemon juice in saucepan. Bring to a boil. Remove from heat and add vanilla. **(24 servings)**

Apple Dumplings

3 12-ounce tubes refrigerated
    buttermilk biscuits
15 medium apples, peeled,
    cored, and halved
$2^1/_2$ cups sugar
2 cups water

1 cup butter or margarine,
    melted
2 teaspoons vanilla
2 teaspoons cinnamon
1 teaspoon nutmeg

Flatten biscuits with hand. Wrap each biscuit around an apple half. Place seam side down in greased baking dishes. Combine sugar, water, butter, and spices. Heat until sugar is dissolved. Remove from heat; add vanilla. Pour over dumplings. Bake, uncovered, at 350 degrees for 35–40 minutes or until golden brown and apples are fork-tender. Serve with vanilla ice cream. **(30 servings)**

Cherry-Cheese Cake

1 package white cake mix
3 8-ounce packages cream
    cheese, softened
5 cups confectioners sugar

1 pint whipping cream,
    whipped
2 21-ounce cans cherry pie
    filling

Prepare cake mix according to package directions. Pour into greased and floured 12x17x1-inch baking pan. Bake at 350 degrees for 20 minutes. Cool. In a mixing bowl, beat cream cheese and sugar until fluffy. Spread over cake and top with cherry pie filling. Chill overnight. **(30 servings)**

How Much for How Many?

Ingredients	For 25 servings	For 50 servings
Dip	3 cups	5 cups
Carrot sticks	3 pounds carrots	6 pounds carrots
Celery sticks	3 pounds celery	6 pounds celery
Tomatoes	15 medium	30 medium
Lettuce, iceburg	4 heads (about 4 pounds)	8 heads (about 8 pounds)
Lettuce, romaine or red leaf	8 heads (about 6 pounds)	16 heads (about 12 pounds)
Salad dressing, for tossing	3 cups (24 ounces)	6 cups (48 ounces)
Salad dressing, for salad bar (2 ounces per serving)	6 cups (48 ounces)	12 cups (3 quarts)
Watermelon	1 large (about 12 pounds)	2 large (about 24 pounds)
Cantaloupe	2 medium	4 medium
Strawberries	3 1-pint baskets	6 1-pint baskets
Grapes	2 pounds	4 pounds
Butter/margarine (1/2 tablespoon per serving)	3/4 pound (3 cubes)	1 1/2 pounds (6 cubes)
Ice cream	1 to 1 1/2 gallons	2 to 2 1/2 gallons
Topping for ice cream	24 ounces	48 ounces
Whipping cream (2 teaspoons per serving)	1 pint	2 pints

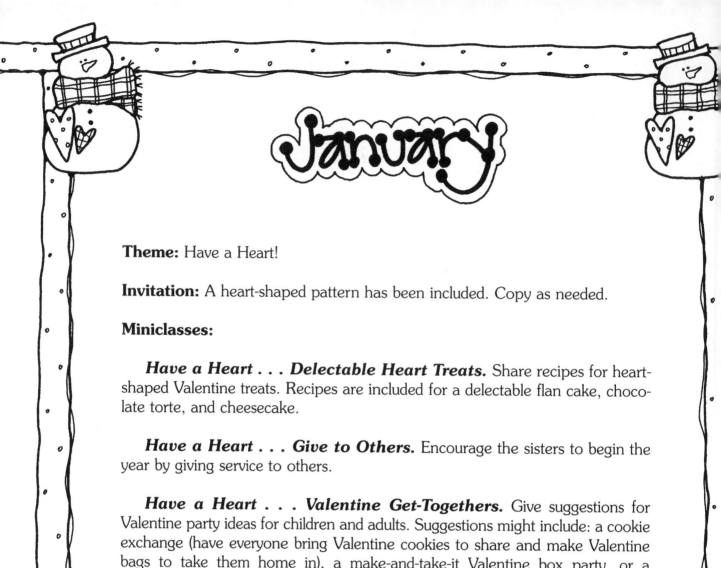

January

Theme: Have a Heart!

Invitation: A heart-shaped pattern has been included. Copy as needed.

Miniclasses:

    Have a Heart . . . Delectable Heart Treats. Share recipes for heart-shaped Valentine treats. Recipes are included for a delectable flan cake, chocolate torte, and cheesecake.

    Have a Heart . . . Give to Others. Encourage the sisters to begin the year by giving service to others.

    Have a Heart . . . Valentine Get-Togethers. Give suggestions for Valentine party ideas for children and adults. Suggestions might include: a cookie exchange (have everyone bring Valentine cookies to share and make Valentine bags to take them home in), a make-and-take-it Valentine box party, or a "Lover's Only" party for adults (have partners secretly make Valentines for each other and make a game of guessing which Valentine belongs to whom).

    Have a Heart . . . Don't Leave Those You Love Heartbroken. Have a qualified financial planner give suggestions on how you can prepare for your family's well-being. Discuss topics such as wills, trusts, insurance, financial planning, and so on, as well as ideas for organizing all of these materials.

Have a Heart . . . Delectable Heart Treats

Flan Cake

1 cake mix, white or yellow
1 can condensed milk
1 8-ounce package cream cheese, softened

$1/3$ cup lemon juice
$1/2$ teaspoon vanilla

Recipe makes 2 cakes. You will need 2 flan cake pans that can be purchased at any specialty cooking store, or you can use round or heart-shaped tart pans. Mix the cake as directed on package, and divide between 2 pans. Bake at temperature specified on package for 10–12 minutes. Cool in pan for 15 minutes. Remove cake from pan and cool. For filling, mix condensed milk, softened cream cheese, lemon juice, and vanilla until smooth. When cake is completely cooled, top with filling and chill. When ready to serve, top with canned cherries or fresh fruits such as strawberries, raspberries, and kiwi.

Tori's Cheesecake

1 8-ounce package cream cheese,
   softened
3 tablespoons milk
1 cup powdered sugar

1 8-ounce container whipped
   topping, thawed
Prepared graham cracker crust

Mix together the cream cheese, milk, and powdered sugar; fold in the whipped topping. Place in graham cracker crust and chill. Top with cherry or blueberry pie filling or fresh fruit and whipped topping. (Thanks to Tori Gerber, Alpine, Utah.)

Carnival Meringue Torte

6 egg whites
1/2 teaspoon salt
1 teaspoon cream of tartar
1 1/2 cups granulated sugar

1 teaspoon almond extract
1 cup finely chopped walnuts
Chocolate Cloud Filling

Several days ahead:

Start heating oven to 300 degrees. Cut 6 8-inch circles from brown paper. In large bowl, with electric mixer at high speed, beat egg whites with salt and cream of tartar until frothy. Add sugar, 2 tablespoons at a time, beating well after each addition until stiff peaks form. Fold in almond extract and nuts.

With spatula, divide meringue mixture in bowl in half; then divide each half into thirds. Spread each of these meringue sixths over one of the brown paper circles.

Bake 2 (or up to 4) of the meringue circles at a time on a large cookie sheet for 40 minutes. Let meringues cool on wire racks (do not remove paper). Cracks are normal in finished meringues.

Carefully wrap cooled meringue circles in plastic wrap and store at room temperature until ready to use.

Day before serving:

Make filling (see recipe below). Carefully remove brown paper from bottom of each meringue circle. Spread filling over 5 of the circles, spreading it to the edges. Stack circles one on top of another. Refrigerate until ready to serve.

Chocolate Cloud Filling

In a double boiler top, over hot (not boiling) water, melt 1 1/2 6-ounce packages (about 1 1/2 cups) semi-sweet chocolate chips until smooth. In a bowl, with electric mixer at medium speed, beat together 1 1/2 8-ounce packages cream cheese, 1 1/2 tablespoons milk, 3/4 cup brown sugar, and a dash of salt until smooth. In a separate bowl, whip 1 1/2 cups heavy or whipping cream until stiff peaks form. Fold in chocolate mixture and 1 1/2 teaspoons vanilla. Fold chocolate mixture into cream cheese mixture and spread onto meringue circles.

Have a Heart . . . Give to Others

Check your local area for homeless shelters, women's shelters, and other organizations that can provide service opportunities and that always welcome donations. Your own ward missionaries serving in other countries also might offer opportunities for service. The Deseret Industries has a program that enables Church groups and members to participate in projects benefiting needy people around the world. For more information on this project, contact: Deseret Industries Sort Center, ATTN: Humanitarian Service, P.O. Box 26393-0393, 1665 Bennett Road, Salt Lake City, Utah 84126-0393. Telephone: 801-240-1940.

Alternative Themes and Miniclasses

Theme: Follow the Prophet

Invitation: Use a small picture of President Gordon B. Hinckley with the proverb "As the twig is bent, so is the tree inclined" attached.

Miniclass:

Begin the new year by following the prophet's counsel on how to strengthen our families and our nation. Have all the sisters meet together, and present the information from the First Presidency Message by President Gordon B. Hinckley, "Four Simple Things to Help Our Families and Our Nations," as found on pages 2–8 of the September 1996 *Ensign*. Have the four members of the Relief Society presidency or other sisters cover the information in each of the four areas: (1) teach your children goodness, (2) work together, (3) read good books together, and (4) pray together. This is such important counsel that homemaking classes could be taught on these subjects throughout the year.

Theme: Search the Scriptures

Invitation: Make a bookmark that includes the scripture-study schedule for the year, and attach homemaking meeting information.

Miniclasses:

Introduction to Scripture Study. Prepare for the new year's scripture study by introducing the year's focus scripture (1998: Old Testament) and discussing ideas for effective study. Have the Spiritual Living or Gospel Doctrine teachers initiate a gospel study program.

Family Home Evening Study. Share ideas for family scripture study and introducing the year's focus scripture to your families. Ideas for scripture study programs for children could be shared.

Teen Values from the Scriptures. Share ideas for involving teens in studying the scriptures and for teaching them values from the scriptures.

Family Home Evening Treats and Games. Share ideas for games and treats that will appeal to all age groups and make family home evening a fun night for everyone.

February

Theme: Get Back to Basics at Homemaking Meeting

Invitation: A form is included which may be copied as needed.

Miniclasses:

The Basics of Cooking. Teach basic cooking techniques for inexperienced cooks or a class on how to teach children or prospective missionaries how to cook.

Everything Comes Out in the Wash . . . or Does It? The Basics of Laundry. Teach basic laundry techniques and how to remove stubborn stains.

The Basics of Quilting. Introduce an ongoing quilting class in which the sisters will learn to make a variety of quilting blocks that can be combined into a small quilt or wall hanging.

The Most Basic Skill of All. Introduce sisters to volunteer possibilities in the community where they can help others attain literacy skills.

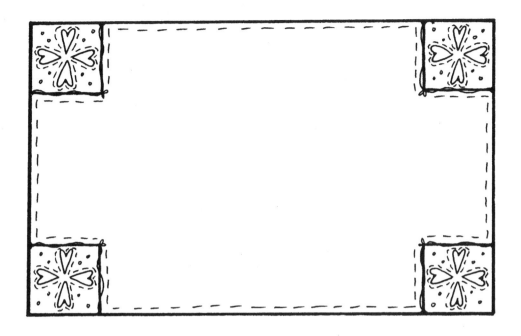

The Basics of Cooking

Cooking is becoming a lost art! Few families have a home-cooked meal more than once a week, and all too often families eat out or bring home fast foods and eat in relays. Many young women marry not knowing how to prepare and serve a balanced, attractive meal. The acquisition of a few basic skills will help the sisters learn how to cook nutritious meals for their families. The *Better Homes and Gardens New Cook Book* (Des Moines, Iowa: Meredith Corporation) is an excellent cookbook for beginning cooks. Have a sister in the ward teach about measuring ingredients, basic cooking terms, and so on.

White Sauces

White sauces are a basic cooking ingredient of many recipes. Most white sauces are made with milk, but broth can also be used as the liquid (chicken broth, beef broth, or the water saved from cooked vegetables). Leftover meats and vegetables can be added to the sauce, and the sauce can be served over cooked pasta. Add a tossed green salad and you have a meal in minutes!

Basic White Sauce

All recipes are for 1 cup of sauce; multiply to make the amount needed.

Thin White Sauce:
    1 tablespoon butter or margarine
    1 tablespoon flour
    1 cup milk

Medium White Sauce:	2 tablespoons butter or margarine
	2 tablespoons flour
	1 cup milk
Thick White Sauce:	3 tablespoons butter or margarine
	3 tablespoons flour
	1 cup milk

Melt butter or margarine in saucepan over medium heat. Blend flour into melted butter. Add *cold* milk all at once and stir constantly until thickened. Add salt and pepper to taste (for a true white sauce, use white pepper instead of black pepper).

The trick to producing a smooth white sauce is to melt the butter at a medium temperature and, after stirring the butter and flour together, to quickly add the cold milk and mix with a wire whisk. If you add warm or hot liquid to the butter/flour mixture, it will be lumpy. To reduce calories in the white sauce, use skim milk.

Everything Comes Out in the Wash . . . or Does It?

If everything doesn't come out in the wash at your house, maybe you are not following the basic rules of laundry.

1. Sort whites, light colors, medium colors, dark colors, towels, garments, and so on. Use a lower water level if batches are smaller rather than combining loads of clothing. Sort heavily soiled clothing from lighter soiled clothing. White clothing will always be dull and dingy if it is combined with colored clothing. Mixing towels with dark socks results in lint-covered towels.

2. Pretreat stains with a commercial stain remover.

3. Don't use too much soap. If water feels slippery, you have enough soap, even if you cannot see suds. Too much soap leaves a residue on the clothing that builds up and makes clothing look dingy.

4. If you live in a hard-water area and do not have a water softener, use a water softening agent along with your soap.

5. Bleach whites to keep them white. Using a very small amount of bleach every time you wash white clothes will keep clothes white. Do not use a large amount of bleach; it will weaken the fabric fibers. (Bleach will turn some nylon fabrics yellow.)

Removing Stains

Check the booklet that came with your washer for a stain removal guide. The recipe below will rejuvenate most dingy white clothing. Do not use on colored clothing.

White Rejuvenator

"She looketh well to the ways of her household" (Proverbs 31:27).

1 gallon very hot water
$1/2$ cup dishwashing detergent (powder)
$1/4$ cup bleach

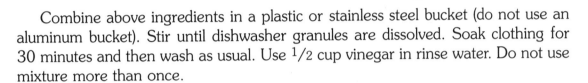

Combine above ingredients in a plastic or stainless steel bucket (do not use an aluminum bucket). Stir until dishwasher granules are dissolved. Soak clothing for 30 minutes and then wash as usual. Use $1/2$ cup vinegar in rinse water. Do not use mixture more than once.

The Basics of Quilting

Quilting is an increasingly popular hobby. Introduce a series of monthly mini-classes in which the sisters will learn to piece traditional quilt blocks. There are numerous basic quilting books on the market that have excellent instructions for piecing and finishing a quilt if you do not have a proficient quilter in your ward who can teach these skills.

Show how to use a rotary cutter and cutting board. Each month for the next four to nine months, learn a new pieced block. Have the sisters in the class pick the blocks they want to learn. A sister who only wants to come to the class for one month could piece the block and use it to make a pillow.

When the blocks are completed, teach how to sew the blocks together with sashing. The sisters should then learn how to put the quilt together. The basic quilting stitch should be taught. Finally, teach how to bind the quilt. A small four-block wall hanging, properly pieced and assembled, could make a lovely addition to a sister's home.

This could also be an opportunity to give service to others. Fabric donated by sisters in the ward could be sewn into plain quilt tops, and the quilts could be quilted or tied and given to a local charity.

The Most Basic Skill of All

Encourage the sisters to seek opportunities to increase literacy in their community. The Relief Society Handbook contains outlines for literacy efforts. Check with priesthood leaders about the Church's gospel literacy guidelines. Check in your community for opportunities available for volunteering to help those who cannot read. Schools, libraries, homeless shelters, and centers for the blind often need volunteers. The following are national literacy groups you might contact:

Literacy Volunteers of America, Inc.
5795 Widewaters Parkway, Dept. P
Syracuse, New York 13214

National Center for Family Literacy
325 West Main Street, Dept. P
Louisville, Kentucky 40202-4251
(502-584-1133)

Alternative Themes and Miniclasses

Theme: Ties That Bind

Invitation: Use a cute recipe card as your invitation. Clip a note to the recipe card inviting the sisters to bring a potluck dish to homemaking meeting. Tell them to use the card to make a copy of their recipe to share with the other sisters. Let them know that it is not mandatory to bring food, since some sisters may not have the time or the finances to do so. Although it may seem to be a good idea to assign categories of dishes—casseroles, salads, desserts—often it is more fun to let everybody bring what they want. So what if everyone brings dessert—have a dessert buffet!

Miniclasses:

Around the Kitchen Table. Use the *Ensign* article titled "A Table Encircled with Love" by Elder LeGrand R. Curtis (May 1995, pp. 82–83) as a guideline for this class.

Family Councils. The lesson titled "Family Councils: A Heavenly Pattern" in the Relief Society lesson manual titled *Follow Me* (Salt Lake City: The Church of Jesus Christ of Latter-day Saints, 1992, pp. 88–92) could be used as a guideline for this miniclass.

Fun Times with Grandparents. Have a grandmother share ideas on activities with grandchildren.

Neighborhood Goodwill. An article titled "Bells Are Ringing" in the February 22, 1997, issue of the *Church News* might be used as a guideline for this miniclass.

Theme: Color Me Happy at Homemaking Meeting

Invitation: Tie each announcement to a crayon.

Miniclasses:

Color Me . . . Yellow. Share recipes for foods using lemon juice.

Color Me . . . Green. Do a Saint Patrick's Day craft project—just be sure it is green!

Color Me . . . Red. Present ideas on the theme "Don't see red; discipline with love."

Color Me . . . Blue. Are you blue? Share ideas for coping with stress and depression.

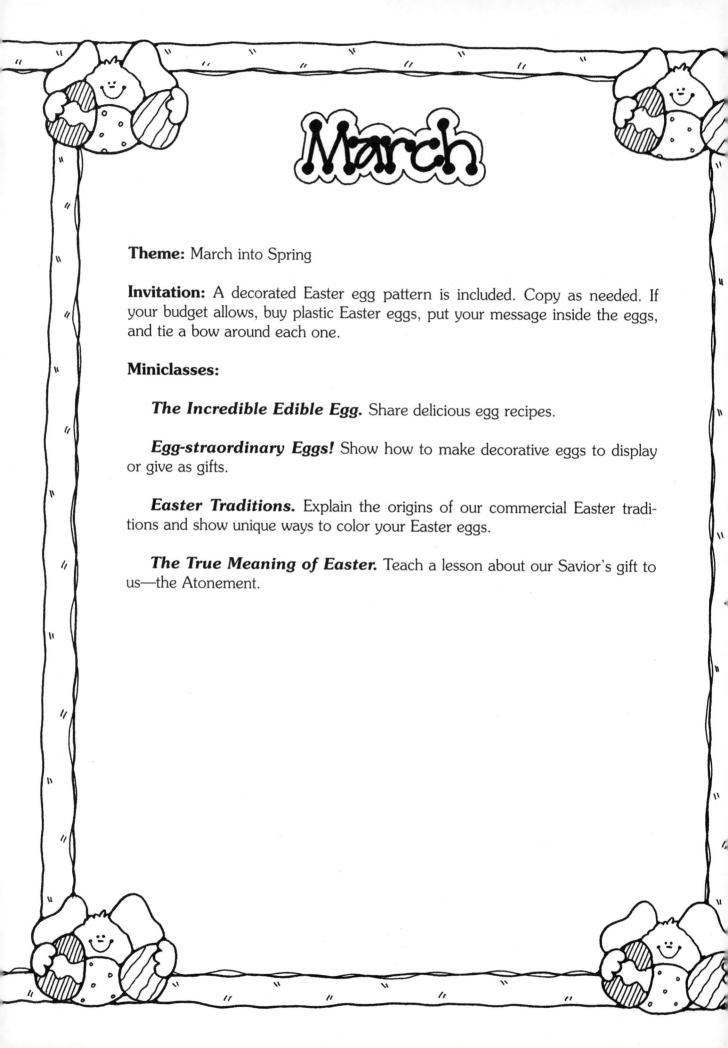

March

Theme: March into Spring

Invitation: A decorated Easter egg pattern is included. Copy as needed. If your budget allows, buy plastic Easter eggs, put your message inside the eggs, and tie a bow around each one.

Miniclasses:

The Incredible Edible Egg. Share delicious egg recipes.

Egg-straordinary Eggs! Show how to make decorative eggs to display or give as gifts.

Easter Traditions. Explain the origins of our commercial Easter traditions and show unique ways to color your Easter eggs.

The True Meaning of Easter. Teach a lesson about our Savior's gift to us—the Atonement.

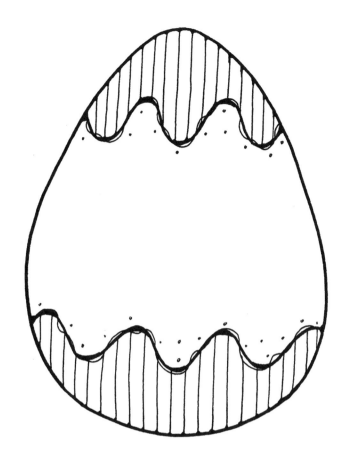

The Incredible Edible Egg

Deviled Egg Casserole

Boil one dozen eggs to hard-boiled stage. (See instructions for perfect hard-boiled eggs in the "Easter Traditions" section.) After eggs are cool, cut in half lengthwise and remove yolks, putting yolks into bowl and setting whites aside to be filled later. Combine yolks, 1/2 cup mayonnaise, 1/2 teaspoon curry, and salt and pepper to taste. Beat with mixer until smooth and creamy. Spoon yolk mixture into whites and place filled eggs in a 9x13x2-inch casserole dish. Cut 2 half-inch ham slices into half-inch cubes. Sprinkle ham cubes over eggs. Pour sauce (recipe below) over eggs and ham. Sprinkle top with buttered bread crumbs, paprika, and dried chives. Bake at 350 degrees for 25 minutes.

Sauce

1/2 cup butter or margarine
1/2 cup flour
4 cups milk
1/2 teaspoon salt

3 cups grated sharp cheddar cheese
1/2 teaspoon dry mustard
1 teaspoon Worcestershire sauce
2 teaspoons very finely chopped onions

Melt butter in saucepan on medium heat. Add flour and stir together. Stir *cold* milk into butter/flour mixture and stir constantly until thickened. Add remaining ingredients, stirring until cheese is melted.

Mystery Casserole

16 slices sandwich bread, cut crusts completely off
4 1/2-inch-thick slices ham, cut into 1/2-inch cubes
1/2 cup finely chopped onions
2 pounds grated sharp cheddar cheese
6 eggs, well beaten

2 1/4 cups milk
1/2 teaspoon dry mustard
Paprika
Dried chives

Fit 8 slices of bread on bottom of greased 9x13x2-inch casserole. Sprinkle with half of the ham cubes, half of the chopped onions, and half of the grated cheese. Layer remaining bread slices, ham, onions, and cheese. Combine eggs, milk, and dry mustard. Pour over layered ingredients. Cover tightly with foil or plastic wrap and store in refrigerator overnight. (It is important to make the casserole the night before.) When ready to bake, sprinkle top of casserole with paprika and dried chives. Bake 1 hour at 300 degrees. You can serve the casserole plain or with a sauce made by diluting a can of mushroom soup with 1 cup water.

Egg-straordinary Eggs!

Use an old paintbrush to coat Styrofoam balls with diluted white glue. Roll or press dried lavender, rose petals, or other dried potpourri to entirely cover egg. Crumple tin foil inside a clay pot to within 1/2 inch of the top. Use a layer of moss on top of pot as a base for the egg. (See illustration.) Tie wired ribbon (1/2- to 1-inch thick, depending on size of egg) around potpourri-covered egg. Anchor ribbon with a straight pin at top and bottom of egg. Tie bow on top of egg. For added support, stick a very thin dowel or barbecue skewer into clay pot and stick egg onto skewer.

Very small pots and eggs could be used as place cards for Easter dinner. Assorted sizes of larger pots would make nice centerpieces for the tables.

Other options:

Eggs could be rolled in spices—poppy seeds, celery seeds, sesame seeds, cinnamon, or allspice. A patchwork spice ball could also be made by painting portions of the egg with diluted glue, pressing on the spices, and allowing to dry. When egg is dry, paint another part of egg and press on another spice. Wrap completed egg with raffia or make a design with whole cloves pressed into the egg.

An elegant egg could be made by pinning tiny silk roses closely together all over a Styrofoam egg. Silk roses are available in packages at most craft stores.

Easter Traditions

The name Easter may have been derived from the name of the ancient Anglo-Saxon goddess of spring, Eostre. The egg was an ancient symbol of new life, and a feast of eggs was used to honor Eostre. Colored eggs were rolled over the fields in the belief that this helped make the earth fertile. Another tradition says that the longing for the colors of spring and summer after the long, cold winter inspired the tradition of coloring eggs.

The Easter bunny also comes from an ancient custom. Legend says that Eostre's favorite animal was a large bird, but one day, when angry with the bird, she changed it into a rabbit. Others say that the bunny is of German origin and has become associated with Easter because he is a symbol of prolific reproduction. In A.D. 325 the Nicene Council decided that Easter should be celebrated on the first Sunday following the full moon after March 21, the spring equinox.

Whatever pagan or man-made customs have become a part of our Easter holiday, the one true meaning of Easter is the celebration of the Atonement of the Savior. We celebrate the Savior's gift to us of the resurrection and everlasting life.

Boiling Perfect Eggs

The best way to boil eggs is to cover the eggs with cold water, bring the water to a full rolling boil, then remove the pan of eggs from the heat and let the eggs sit in the water until the water cools. By the time the water is cool, the eggs will be hard-cooked, and generally there will not be a dark rim around the yolk.

Egg Boiling and Coloring Tips

1. To ensure that the shells will come smoothly off your hard-cooked eggs, buy your eggs early and let them sit a week or 10 days in the refrigerator. Very fresh eggs do not peel easily.

2. Puncture the large end of the eggshell with a needle just before cooking to keep eggs from cracking.

3. Handle eggs as little as possible before dyeing. The oil from your hands will resist the dye.

4. Wipe the eggs off with vinegar to remove blemishes and scratches.

5. If you add 2 tablespoons of vinegar to the water before cooking eggs, the egg white from cracked eggs will not leak into the water.

Coloring Easter Eggs

Instead of using store-bought colors, try coloring your eggs with natural dyes. Prepare the eggs for dyeing by first washing them to remove the oil coating; the dye will adhere better. Use onion skins (red or yellow), raspberries, grass, spinach leaves, red cabbage, blueberries, raw beets, cherries, saffron, or tumeric, or experiment with other fresh vegetables and fruits from your produce counter. To dye eggs, place eggs in a pan along with 1 or 2 cups of the natural dyeing materials, cover with water, and add 1 tablespoon vinegar. Simmer eggs for 15 minutes and then leave in pan for 1 hour. When dry, brush with cooking oil. The natural dyes will make lovely, soft colors.

To make beautiful natural designs on cooked eggs, choose small leaves and flowers (if the leaves are stiff, dip them quickly into hot water to make them limp), hold the plants against the egg, and wrap the egg tightly in an old nylon stocking. Secure the stocking with rubber bands. Dip the eggs into the dyes and leave in dye until desired color is attained.

Other Egg Decorating Ideas

Make plaid eggs by putting rubber bands on the egg before dying.

To make tie-dyed eggs, wrap the egg in fabric and secure the ends with rubber bands or twist ties. Soak in dye and let dry overnight. Remove the cloth.

Wax-resist eggs can be made using candle wax. Burn a votive candle in a small votive holder until melted wax forms around the wick. Stick straight pins, corsage pins, glass headed pins, etc., into the erasers of pencils and use these pins dipped in melted wax in the same way you would dip-dot paint with acrylics. You could also use the pencil eraser itself as a large dot. Use toothpicks or an old paintbrush to draw designs on the egg with the melted wax. Dip the eggs into the dyes. To remove the wax after dyeing, place the egg in a warm oven until the wax begins to melt, then wipe away with a paper towel. You can also remove the wax with de-natured alcohol, cleaning fluid, or rubber cement thinner. An old-fashioned pen-holder with a metal nib makes a wonderful drawing tool.

Make beautiful marbled eggs. Fill a cup $2/3$ full of boiling water. Add 1 teaspoon food coloring and 1 teaspoon vinegar. Fill several cups, using a different color in each cup. Add 1 teaspoon vegetable oil to each mug. Before dyeing eggs, cover your work surface with paper towels. Stir water vigorously; place an egg on a spoon and immediately dip egg in and out of dye (dip just once). Place egg on paper towel to dry. Restir dye before dipping another egg. The oil will prevent the dye from covering the entire egg. The more the oil has been stirred, the more marbled the egg will be. After the eggs have dried, you can redip the egg in 1 or 2 colors. When finished, wipe off excess oil with paper towel.

The True Meaning of Easter

Review a book about the Atonement of the Savior. You might also check with the ward librarian for an appropriate video that could be shown and discussed. Check copies of the *Ensign,* especially the May issue, for a conference talk that could be used as a guide for your miniclass. Be sure to allow time during the class for testimonies from sisters who are willing to share their personal feelings about the Atonement.

Alternative Themes and Miniclasses

Theme: Be a Lifesaver. (March is Red Cross month. Teach the sisters how to deal with emergencies.)

Invitation: Glue a LifeSaver candy on your message.

Miniclasses:

Good Health Through Eating Correctly. Teach a class on fat-free and sugarless cooking.

Basic First Aid. Have a paramedic or nurse from your ward teach the class.

Emergency Kits. Demonstrate what is needed in a basic emergency kit, or have the sisters put a kit together in class. Or do a service project by putting together a first-aid kit for the Deseret Industries Sort Center (be sure to check guidelines before making the kits).

Home Nursing. Have a nurse teach a class on caring for the bedridden patient in the home.

Theme: Your Lucky Day . . . at Homemaking Meeting

Invitation: Use a shamrock cutout for your invitation—green, of course!

Miniclasses:

Emerald Isle Cooking. Use recipes for corned beef, Irish soda bread, potato casseroles.

Let's Go Fly a Kite. Teach how to make a basic kite. Encourage the sisters to make kites for family night and then go fly the kites as a family. A wonderful memory for children!

Celebrate Crafts! March is National Craft Month. Select a spring craft project—perhaps a spring grapevine wreath for the front door.

Make Someone's Day Lucky! Do a service project or make an item that can be donated to the sort center. Check guidelines.

Theme: Thyme for . . . Homemaking!

Invitation: A flowerpot invitation pattern is included. Copy as needed. You might want to use a few sprigs of fresh herbs, if available, and attach home-making information with a ribbon or raffia.

Miniclasses:

Thyme for . . . Growing Herbs. Have a class on growing herbs, and start herb gardens by planting herb baskets to take home.

Thyme for . . . Cooking with Herbs. Learn to use herbs in your cook-ing. Share recipes using a variety of herbs. An herb cooking chart is included. Also included are instructions for making herb brushes used in flavoring grilled foods, as well as instructions for herb butter logs.

Thyme for . . . Spring Cleaning. Learn how to efficiently clean and organize your home, and share tips for top-to-bottom spring cleaning. There are many books available that can be used as resources. Eugenia Chapman and Jill C. Major share their cleaning expertise in *Clean Your House and Every-thing in It* (New York: Perigee Books, 1991). Don Aslett has several profes-sional cleaning books, including *Is There Life after Housework?* (Cincinnati: Writer's Digest Books, 1985), *Do I Dust or Vacuum First?* (Cincinnati: Writer's Digest Books, 1982), *Make Your House Do the Housework* (Cincinnati: Writer's Digest Books, 1986), and *500 Terrific Ideas for Cleaning Everything* (New York: Simon and Schuster, 1991).

Thyme for . . . Clay Pots. Be creative in using clay pots to show off herbs and plants and in decorating your home. Clay pots can be decorated with seeds, shells, dried flowers, or acrylic paints. Clay pot saucers, sponge-painted and filled with potpourri, can add a fun, decorative touch. Have each sister dec-orate her own clay pot to take home.

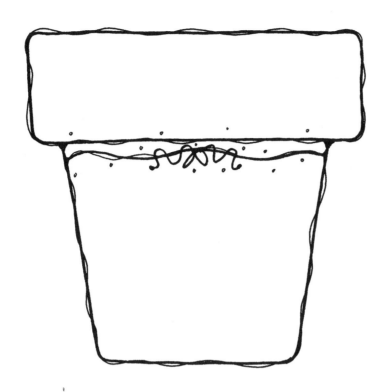

Thyme for . . . Cooking with Herbs

Herb	Uses
Basil	Green, potato, and tomato salads; salad dressings; breads; egg dishes; dips; marinades; sauces; tomatoes; squash; pasta; broiled and roasted meats; poultry pies; stews; stuffing; and baked, broiled, or poached fish.
Bay Leaf	Seafood cocktails, tomato aspic, egg dishes, gravies, marinades, sauces, beets, carrots, onions, potatoes, rice, squash, corned beef, poultry stews, shellfish, and fish stews.
Chives	Green, potato, and tomato salads; salad dressings; egg and cheese dishes; cream cheese; cottage cheese; gravies; sauces; potatoes; broiled poultry; poultry and meat pies; stews; casseroles; baked fish; and fish stews.
Dill	Seafood cocktail, salad dressings, breads, egg and cheese dishes, cream cheese, beans, beets, cabbage, carrots, peas, squash, tomatoes, beef, veal, lamb, steaks, chops, stews, fish, shellfish, and tuna fish.
Garlic	All salads, salad dressings, poultry sauces, marinades, pastas, beans, eggplant, potatoes, tomatoes, rice, roast meats, hamburgers, stews, casseroles, broiled fish, and shellfish.

27

Herb	Uses
Marjoram	Green and seafood salads, breads, cheese spreads, egg and cheese dishes, gravies, carrots, eggplant, peas, onions, potatoes, spinach, roast meats, poultry, stews, casseroles, and baked or broiled fish.
Mustard	Green salads, macaroni and potato salads, salad dressings, biscuits, egg and cheese dishes, baked beans, cabbage, squash, dried beans, mushrooms, pasta, chops, steaks, ham, pork, poultry, cold meats, and shellfish.
Oregano	Green and seafood salads, breads, egg and cheese dishes, cabbage, artichokes, squash, dried beans, mushrooms, pasta, meat loaf, meat and poultry pies, stews, casseroles, stuffing, and fish stews.
Parsley	Green, potato, and seafood salads; biscuits; breads; egg and cheese dishes; gravies; sauces; asparagus; beets; mushrooms; pasta; meat loaf; meat and poultry pies; stews; casseroles; stuffing; and fish stews.
Rosemary	Fruit cocktail, fruit and green salads, biscuits, egg dishes, herb butter, cream cheese, marinades, sauces, beans, broccoli, peas, cauliflower, mushrooms, baked potatoes, parsnips, roast meat, poultry, stews, casseroles, stuffing, and shellfish.
Sage	Breads, fondue, egg and cheese dishes, spreads, gravies, sauces, beans, beets, onions, peas, spinach, tomatoes, roast meat, poultry, meat loaf, stews, stuffing, and baked fish.
Thyme	Seafood cocktail, green and seafood salads, biscuits, breads, egg and cheese dishes, sauces, spreads, beets, carrots, mushrooms, onions, peas, eggplant, spinach, potatoes, roast meat, poultry, meat loaf, stews, casseroles, and baked or broiled fish.

Herb Brushes

Tie freshly picked bunches of herb sprigs together with a piece of twine. Dip in olive or vegetable oil and use to baste grilled foods such as chicken, fish, steaks, or vegetables. Excellent herbs to use for basting are: cilantro, thyme, sage, oregano, dill, chives, basil, parsley, rosemary, and mint.

Herb and Butter Logs

Mix fresh, crushed herbs with softened sweet butter and roll into logs or desired shapes with waxed paper or parchment paper; chill until hardened. Slice and serve. Can use any combination of herbs desired.

Alternative Themes and Miniclasses

Theme: Springtime Potpourri

Invitation: Write homemaking information on a pretty colored envelope, fill with a small amount of potpourri, seal envelope, and attach a ribbon or dried flowers.

Miniclasses:

Potpourri Scents. Learn how to make your own potpourri using flowers and herbs from your garden. *Better Homes and Gardens Floral and Nature Crafts,* a magazine published by Meredith Corporation, often has ideas for potpourri and materials to be used.

A Potpourri of Flavors. Have a class sharing recipes for a variety of different casseroles. Casseroles could be used for the luncheon following the classes.

Potpourri Topiary. Topiaries placed in small clay pots can be made by using purchased potpourri, lavender, small rosebuds, herbs, or other desired materials. Coat Styrofoam ball with white glue, roll in potpourri, or press potpourri onto ball with fingers. (See *Homemaking Blueprints,* vol. 1, p. 34, for further instructions.)

A Potpourri of Service. Present a variety of service opportunities that might be available, or use the time to work on a service project.

Theme: Especially for Mom

Invitation: Attach information to a pretty doily.

Miniclasses:

Treats a Mother Will Love . . . Muffins. Share recipes for a variety of muffins.

Mother's Apron Strings. Make an apron for Mother for Mother's Day.

A Day Off . . . Don't Overlook Yourself. Discuss the importance of taking time for yourself, and ideas on how to do it.

A Mother's Story. Review the book *The Revised and Enhanced History of Joseph Smith by His Mother* (Scot Facer Proctor and Maurine Jensen Proctor, eds. [Salt Lake City: Bookcraft, 1996]).

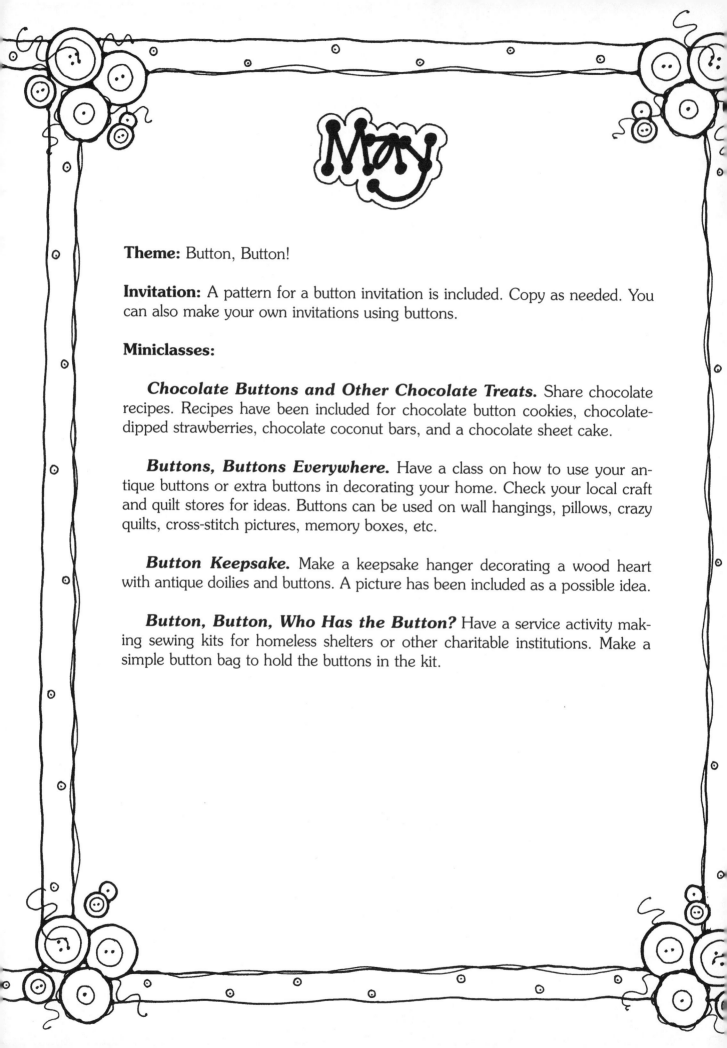

Theme: Button, Button!

Invitation: A pattern for a button invitation is included. Copy as needed. You can also make your own invitations using buttons.

Miniclasses:

Chocolate Buttons and Other Chocolate Treats. Share chocolate recipes. Recipes have been included for chocolate button cookies, chocolate-dipped strawberries, chocolate coconut bars, and a chocolate sheet cake.

Buttons, Buttons Everywhere. Have a class on how to use your antique buttons or extra buttons in decorating your home. Check your local craft and quilt stores for ideas. Buttons can be used on wall hangings, pillows, crazy quilts, cross-stitch pictures, memory boxes, etc.

Button Keepsake. Make a keepsake hanger decorating a wood heart with antique doilies and buttons. A picture has been included as a possible idea.

Button, Button, Who Has the Button? Have a service activity making sewing kits for homeless shelters or other charitable institutions. Make a simple button bag to hold the buttons in the kit.

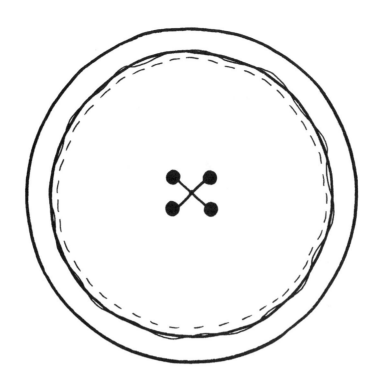

Chocolate Buttons and Other Chocolate Treats

Chocolate button cookies could be made using the sugar cookie recipe in volume 1 of *Homemaking Blueprints* (p. 17) and adding cocoa to the recipe. Use a round cookie cutter and cut small pieces of a drinking straw to make holes in the button cookie. Leave straws in while baking and remove when cool.

Button cookies may also be made by dipping white sugar cookies in chocolate. Tie a 1/8″–1/4″ piece of ribbon through the holes to look like thread (knot on top), if desired.

Chocolate-Dipped Strawberries

3 ounces milk chocolate
3 ounces white chocolate
2 teaspoons vegetable oil

14 large strawberries
Assorted sprinkles, chopped nuts, etc.

Melt milk chocolate and 1 teaspoon oil in a dish in a microwave oven at 100% power for 1 minute; stir until smooth. Melt the white chocolate and 1 teaspoon oil in same manner. Dip half of the strawberries in the milk chocolate and half in the white chocolate. Roll in sprinkles, nuts, and so on, if desired, or decorate with remaining chocolate as follows: Spoon remaining melted chocolate in 2 small plastic bags; snip off 1 corner of each bag. Pipe chocolate over strawberries. Place on waxed paper and chill to harden, about 30 minutes.

Chocolate Coconut Bars

Cover bottom of a 9x13x2-inch pan with prepared graham cracker crust (see below). Spread coconut over the crust and pour a can of Eagle Brand condensed milk over the top. Cook in a 350-degree oven until mixture bubbles. Cover the top with chocolate chips and cook until melted. Cool just enough to cut into squares. Cut and enjoy.

Crust

1^1/3 cups graham cracker crumbs (about 16 crackers)
1/4 cup granulated sugar
1/4 cup margarine or butter (melted)

Mix all ingredients with fork or spoon. Press mixture into bottom of 9x13x2-inch pan.

Joan's Fudge Cake

2 cups sugar   1/2 teaspoon salt
2 cups flour   2 teaspoons cinnamon

Mix above ingredients together in bowl.
In a heavy pan, mix 1 stick butter or margarine, 1/2 cup oil, 1/4 cup cocoa, and 1 cup water. Bring to a boil. Remove from heat and pour over the flour mixture; mix well. In another bowl, mix 1 teaspoon soda in 1/2 cup buttermilk. Add 2 eggs and 1 teaspoon vanilla. Mix well and add to above mixture.
Grease and flour a jelly roll pan or cookie sheet and pour cake onto sheet. Bake for 20 minutes at 400 degrees. While cake is baking, mix frosting.

Frosting

In a large pan, melt 1 stick butter or margarine and add 6–7 teaspoons canned evaporated milk and 4 teaspoons cocoa. Boil. Remove from heat and add 1 16-ounce box powdered sugar, 1 teaspoon vanilla, 1 cup nuts, and a little canned milk to thin. Remove the cake from the oven when done and immediately spread the frosting over the cake (must be done while both are still hot). Let cool.

Button Keepsake

Paint a purchased wooden heart in any desired color. (Use acrylic, water-based paint, or stain, whatever desired.) When dry, decorate the heart with doilies, buttons, jewelry, and so on. Drill 2 holes in top of heart (as on illustration). Thread wire through holes to desired length. Curl ends of wire around a pencil, if desired.

Alternative Themes and Miniclasses

Theme: A Tisket, a Tasket . . . We Love Baskets!

Invitation: Use a small basket with homemaking information attached.

Miniclasses:

Veggie Baskets. Share vegetable and dip recipes and serve in baskets.

Gift Baskets. Have a class with ideas on how to put together gift baskets for various occasions such as weddings, baby showers, bridal showers, and birthdays.

Decorating with Baskets. Share ideas on decorating with baskets that can be not only fun but functional. Use baskets for holding soaps, towels, kitchen items, filing papers, sewing materials, and so on.

Friendshipping Baskets. Have a class on how to friendship members and nonmembers. Use the books *Hasten My Work* by Robert B. Wells (Salt Lake City: Bookcraft, 1996) or *From Conversion to Commitment* by Peggy St. Cyr (Salt Lake City: Bookcraft, 1996) as helps for the class.

Theme: For the Birds!

Invitation: Attach information to a small birdhouse.

Miniclasses:

"Bird" Food. Share recipes for cooking with chicken, turkey, and Cornish game hens.

Birdhouses. Paint a purchased wood birdhouse.

Bird Gardening. Learn how to grow gardens that attract hummingbirds and butterflies.

"Don't Be an Old Bird." Have a class on how to grow old gracefully.

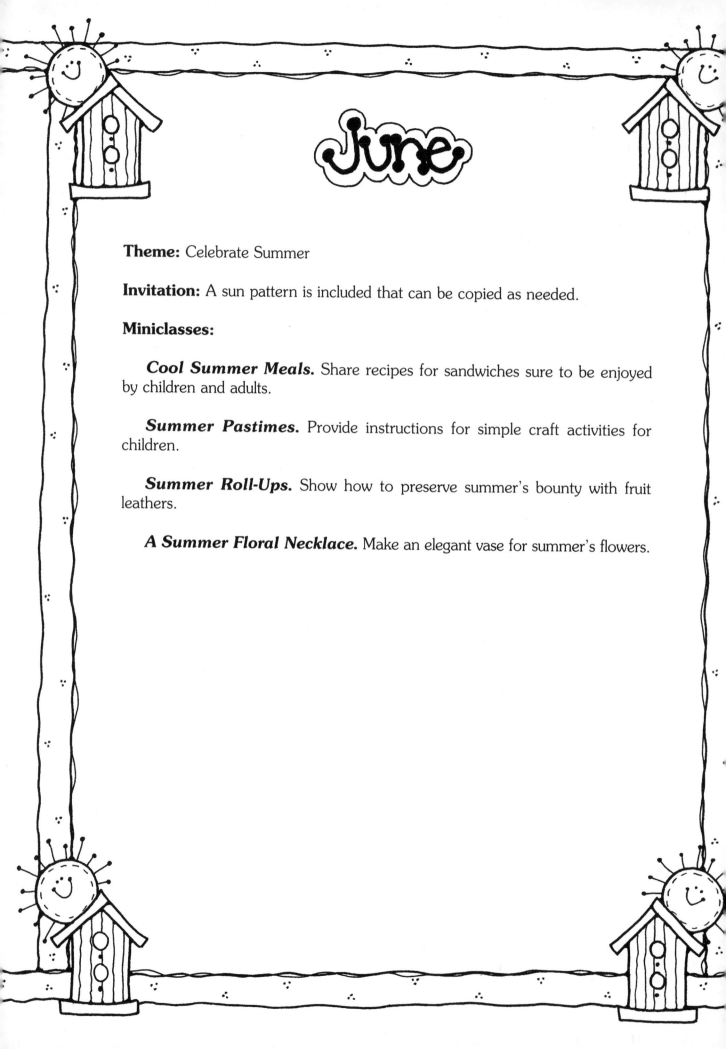

June

Theme: Celebrate Summer

Invitation: A sun pattern is included that can be copied as needed.

Miniclasses:

Cool Summer Meals. Share recipes for sandwiches sure to be enjoyed by children and adults.

Summer Pastimes. Provide instructions for simple craft activities for children.

Summer Roll-Ups. Show how to preserve summer's bounty with fruit leathers.

A Summer Floral Necklace. Make an elegant vase for summer's flowers.

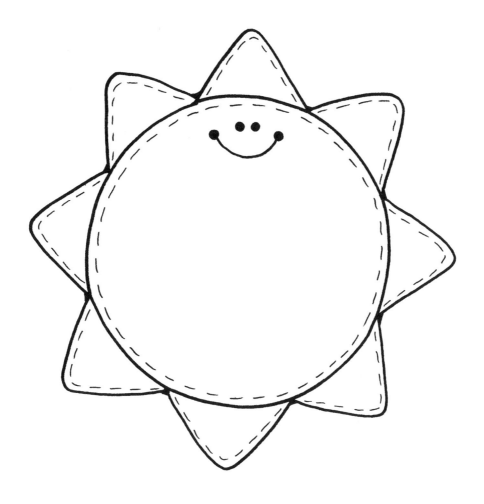

Cool Summer Meals

Sandwiches are the perfect summer meal—quick and easy to fix, and no need to heat the oven! Included are fun roll-up sandwiches that children will love to make and eat, as well as recipes for more elegant sandwich fillings that will appeal to adults.

Yummy Roll-Ups

Place a flour tortilla on a square of plastic wrap. Spread the tortilla with salad dressing or mayonnaise, then salsa, and top with very thinly sliced ham, turkey, or beef. Sprinkle on shredded cheese and lettuce. Roll up, securing plastic wrap with tape if necessary. Refrigerate for 1 hour or more before serving.

Variation: Spread the tortilla with ranch dressing and top with very thin slices of ham, turkey, or beef, and very thin slices of your favorite cheese. Sprinkle with lettuce, sliced olives, and sliced green onions. Roll and refrigerate as above.

Super-Duper Sandwich

Cut a large loaf of French bread in half and scoop out bread to make a cavity for the fillings. Sprinkle inside of cavity with a few drops of balsamic vinegar and a generous amount of olive oil. Salt and pepper to taste. Inside the cavity, layer ingredients of your choice, such as thinly sliced tomatoes, cheese, meat slices, lettuce, grated carrots, thinly sliced green peppers, sliced hard-boiled eggs, thinly sliced red onions, and sliced cucumbers. Between every few layers, spoon on mayonnaise or salad dressing. Wrap the loaf tightly in plastic wrap and refrigerate until ready to serve. Cut in wedges. Serves 8.

Yummy Sandwich Fillings

Egg Filling: Chop 8 hard-cooked eggs into small pieces (about $1/4$ to $1/2$ inch). Add $1/2$ teaspoon prepared mustard, $1/4$ cup mayonnaise, salt to taste, and $1^1/2$ tablespoons chopped chives. Combine and refrigerate.

Deviled Ham Filling: Combine 1 $4^1/2$-ounce can deviled ham, $1/2$ cup finely chopped sweet pickles, 3 tablespoons finely chopped celery, 2 8-ounce packages cream cheese (room temperature), 3 tablespoons mayonnaise, and 1 teaspoon very finely chopped green onions. Blend well and refrigerate.

Crab Filling: Combine 1 cup crab meat, 3 chopped hard-cooked eggs, $1/2$ cup finely chopped celery, 1 teaspoon chives (fresh or dried), 1 teaspoon Worcestershire sauce, $1/2$ cup mayonnaise, and a dash of paprika. Blend well and refrigerate.

Chicken Filling: Combine $1^1/2$ cups chopped cooked chicken, $1/2$ cup finely chopped celery, $1/2$ cup finely chopped fresh mushrooms, $1^1/2$ tablespoons fresh chives (2 teaspoons dried), $1/4$ teaspoon curry powder, $1^1/2$ teaspoons lemon juice, $1/2$ cup mayonnaise, and salt and pepper to taste. Blend well and refrigerate.

Fun Party Idea: Wrap your sandwiches in waxed paper, secure with tape, and put a decorative label on top of the sandwich.

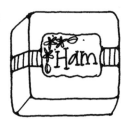

Summer Pastimes

Children love craft activities! And they love to have Mother do the activities with them. Following are some simple recipes for craft materials that can be made at home.

Clay Dough

Food coloring
3 tablespoons salad oil
1 3/4 cups boiling water
2 1/2 cups flour

1/2 cup salt
1 tablespoon alum (this ingredient should be available at the drugstore)

Add food coloring and salad oil to the boiling water. Combine flour, salt, and alum. Pour liquid over dry ingredients; mix together. Cool until clay dough can be handled comfortably; knead until smooth. Store in plastic bag.

Modeling Clay

1 cup salt
1 cup boiling water
Food coloring

2 cups flour
2 tablespoons cornstarch

Mix salt, boiling water, and food coloring together and stir until salt is dissolved. Sift flour and cornstarch. Gradually add water mixture to dry ingredients. Mix well. Knead until smooth. If mixture is too soft, add flour to desired consistency.

Finger Paint #1

1 quart boiling water
1 cup soap flakes (Ivory brand)
1 cup cornstarch

Mix all ingredients together and boil until thick. Add poster paint or food coloring.

Finger Paint #2

1 cup flour
1 cup sugar
6 cups cold water

Mix flour and sugar; stir well. Add water. Cook on low heat, stirring constantly, until thick. Add food coloring.

Grow a Crystal Garden

With a hammer, break up a piece of coal or a common brick into small pieces—about the size of walnuts. Place pieces in an 8x8x2-inch glass casserole dish or a similar bowl with low sides. Don't overcrowd. Pour liquid solution (recipe below) over coal. With a medicine dropper, drop several colors of food coloring over stones. Rinse the dropper in between colors so that colors do not blend. Within a few hours, the crystal garden will "grow" and assume fascinating shapes. Do not move the bowl around after it starts to "grow," since the crystals are very fragile and will break easily. The crystals will continue growing for several days and last for weeks.

Solution: Mix together in order given.

4 tablespoons table salt (noniodized)
4 tablespoons liquid bluing (check laundry aisle in grocery store)
4 tablespoons water
1 tablespoon household ammonia

Summer Roll-Ups

Use fully ripe fruit. Wash and cut away blemishes. Measure (see below for amounts), using about 5 pints fruit for 1 batch of leather. Add sugar and heat to just below a full rolling boil. Remove from heat and pour part of mixture into a blender or food processor; process until smooth. Process balance of fruit. Cool until lukewarm. Pour puree onto jelly roll pan which has been lined with plastic wrap (fasten plastic wrap together with tape so that puree cannot run through the plastic). To keep the fruit clean during drying process, cover with a sheet of cheese-cloth, pulling tightly and taping in place so that it does not touch the puree. Place the fruit leather in full sunlight and let dry for 20–24 hours. Bring in at night and return to dry in the sun the next morning. When leather is firm to the touch, try pulling the plastic wrap away from fruit; if it comes away without leaving traces of fruit, it is ready. Roll up sheets in plastic wrap on which it has dried, then wrap in another layer of plastic wrap and seal tightly. Will keep well for a month at room temperature, 4 months if refrigerated, and a year if frozen.

Apricots: $1^1/2$ tablespoons sugar to 1 cup cut-up apricots.
Strawberries: 1 tablespoon sugar to 1 cup sliced strawberries.
Raspberries: $1^1/2$ tablespoons sugar to 1 cup raspberries (strain seeds from puree
    before blending).
Blackberries: $2^1/2$ tablespoons sugar to 1 cup blackberries.
Peaches: $1^1/2$ tablespoons sugar to 1 cup peeled and sliced peaches.
Plums: $2^1/2$ tablespoons sugar to 1 cup Santa Rosa plums. For other varieties of
    plums, use $1^1/2$ tablespoons sugar to 1 cup sliced plums.
Nectarines: $1^1/2$ tablespoons sugar to 1 cup peeled and sliced nectarines.

Note: If fruit does not dry completely in sun in 24 hours, dry in oven at 140–150 degrees. Leave oven door open while drying to allow moisture to escape.

A Summer Floral Necklace

Materials needed:

Clear glass vase (shaped as in diagram)
1-inch ribbon, enough to tie around neck of vase
Spanish moss
Assorted dried flowers and foliage
Grapevine tendrils (optional)

Check your local thrift shop for inexpensive flower vases. Each vase should have a definite neck indentation. Florists will also stock vases; prices will vary. Sisters may have vases, but be sure to stress that the vase must have a neck indentation.

Wrap the ribbon around the neck of the vase and tie in place. Cut off ends of ribbon. Glue Spanish moss on top of the ribbon. This is your base for the dried flowers. Using a glue gun, glue the dried flowers onto the moss. Vary the size, shape, and color of the flowers and foliage. Add grapevine tendrils.

Alternative Themes and Miniclasses

Theme: The Lazy, Hazy Days of Summer

Invitation: Use the sun pattern for your invitation.

Miniclasses:

Relax with a Fruit Smoothy. Teach how to prepare this fun treat for children and adults.

Relax with a Good Book. Encourage reading of the classics. Get a reading list of classic novels from your local library or have the sisters in the ward share lists of their favorite books.

Relax with Needlework. Have a class in beginning cross-stitch or ribbon embroidery.

Relax! Stop Stress in Its Tracks. Teach how to reduce stress in your life.

Theme: Rally Round the Flag

Invitation: Use tiny toothpick flags (available at your local novelty shop) on your invitation.

Miniclasses:

Patriotic Flag Cake. Frost a 9x12-inch sheet cake with white frosting. Decorate with sliced strawberries for stripes and blueberries for the field of blue.

Make a Family Flag. Research family crest if available or use motifs that have meaning to your family.

A History of the Flag. Give a presentation on the background and evolution of the American flag.

A Flag Welcome. Paint a simple wooden flag decoration for the front door. Hang with a wire hanger, curling the ends of the wire and tying a bow around one side of the wire.

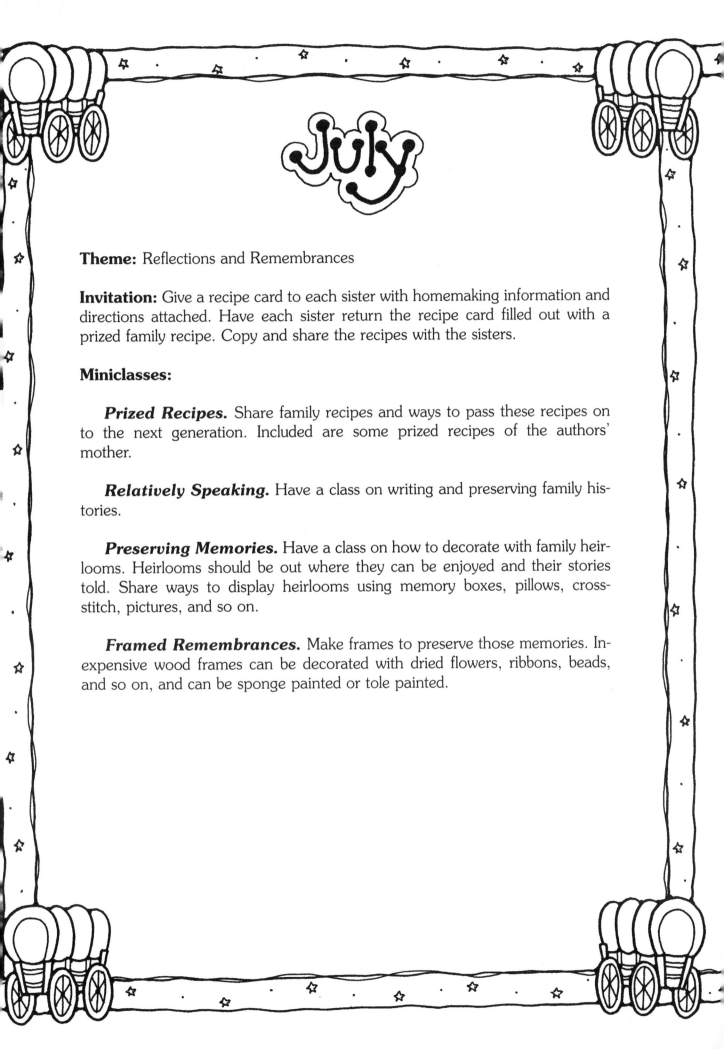

July

Theme: Reflections and Remembrances

Invitation: Give a recipe card to each sister with homemaking information and directions attached. Have each sister return the recipe card filled out with a prized family recipe. Copy and share the recipes with the sisters.

Miniclasses:

Prized Recipes. Share family recipes and ways to pass these recipes on to the next generation. Included are some prized recipes of the authors' mother.

Relatively Speaking. Have a class on writing and preserving family histories.

Preserving Memories. Have a class on how to decorate with family heirlooms. Heirlooms should be out where they can be enjoyed and their stories told. Share ways to display heirlooms using memory boxes, pillows, cross-stitch, pictures, and so on.

Framed Remembrances. Make frames to preserve those memories. Inexpensive wood frames can be decorated with dried flowers, ribbons, beads, and so on, and can be sponge painted or tole painted.

Prized Recipes

Mom's Lemon Icebox Dessert

3 eggs
Juice from 1 1/2 lemons
Grated rind of 1 lemon

2/3 cup sugar
1 cup whipping cream, whipped
Vanilla wafers

Beat egg yolks and add lemon juice, rind, and sugar; cook in a double boiler until thick. Remove from heat and cool. Beat cream and egg whites separately and then fold together. Add cooled custard mixture to cream and egg mixture and blend well. Place a layer of crushed vanilla wafers in the bottom of a 9x13x2-inch pan. Cover with custard filling and top with more crushed vanilla wafers. Freeze.

Mom's Fruit Cup

3/4 cup sugar
1 cup water
3 bananas
3 oranges, peeled and sectioned,
  or use canned mandarin oranges

1 cup crushed pineapple
Juice from one lemon
7 UP or Sprite
Other fruits such as strawberries or grapes
  can be added as desired

Dissolve sugar in water. Cut up bananas and other fruits; combine with pineapple and lemon juice. Add to sugar and water mixture. Mix well. Place in any freezer containers and freeze. When ready to serve, allow to thaw until mushy. Place in individual bowls and cover with 7 UP or Sprite.

Mom's Pear Sea-Foam Salad

1 16-ounce can pears
1 3-ounce package lime gelatin
2 3-ounce packages cream cheese, softened

1 cup whipping cream
1/2 cup chopped pecans (optional)

Drain juice from pears into measuring cup; add water to make 1 cup liquid. Heat liquid in saucepan until almost boiling; remove from heat and add gelatin. Stir until gelatin is dissolved. Chill until gelatin is the consistency of syrup—will coat spoon (about 30 minutes). Check frequently; do not let the gelatin set. When gelatin is chilled, pour into blender with drained pears and puree until smooth. Add cream cheese to mixture in blender and puree until smooth. Whip cream until it holds peaks. Fold in lime mixture. Add pecans. Pour into mold or casserole dish.

Alternative Themes and Miniclasses

Theme: Be a Kid . . . with Your Kids!

Invitation: Attach homemaking information to a blown-up balloon.

July is a good month for mothers and children to have a fun day together. Plan a day at the park or church with games both can enjoy. Children love to play relay games with their mothers, especially water games. This could be a joint activity, having the Primary in charge of the games. Simple prizes could be given to winners. Other activities such as simple crafts and face painting could also be done. Have a potluck luncheon or have each family bring their own sack lunches. Have the Relief Society provide drinks and ice cream bars for dessert.

Theme: Get Up and Go!

Invitation: Attach homemaking information to a cut-out of a walking shoe.

This activity could be for sisters only or for sisters and children. Start early in the morning with breakfast and then go on a hike together. For those sisters who can't or choose not to participate in the hike, provide a book review or a Church video.

August

Theme: Sun-Drenched Days

Invitation: A sunflower pattern is included; copy as needed.

Miniclasses:

   Tangy Homemade Salad Dressings. Show how to make homemade salad dressings to top your summer salads.

   Savory Herb Vinegars. Show how to make your own herb vinegars with fresh herbs from the garden.

   Fragrant Potpourri Doorknob Hanger. Enjoy making this inexpensive and simple project.

   "This Old House." Teach simple home repairs. Make a toolbox that is just for Mom.

Tangy Homemade Salad Dressings

Thousand Island Dressing

1 cup mayonnaise
1 cup salad dressing
1 1/2 cups thick chili sauce

1 1/2 tablespoons finely chopped onion
1 hard-boiled egg, finely chopped

Mix all ingredients together. Blend well. Store in refrigerator. Keeps for several weeks.

Blue Cheese Dressing

6 ounces blue cheese or Roquefort cheese, crumbled
2 cups mayonnaise
1 cup (8 ounces) sour cream
1 1/2 tablespoons vegetable oil
2 tablespoons vinegar

1 teaspoon garlic salt
1 teaspoon onion salt
1/2 teaspoon salt
1 teaspoon pepper

Blend all ingredients in a blender until smooth. Cover and refrigerate.

Italian Dressing

1 1/3 cups olive oil
1/2 cup red wine vinegar
1/4 cup dry grated Parmesan cheese
1/2 teaspoon salt
1 teaspoon celery salt

1/2 teaspoon white pepper
1/2 teaspoon dry mustard
1/4 teaspoon paprika
1 clove garlic, minced

Combine all ingredients in a jar with a tight-fitting lid. Shake until well mixed. Refrigerate.

Poppy Seed Dressing

3/4 cup sugar
1 1/2 teaspoons onion salt
1 teaspoon dry mustard

1/3 cup vinegar
1 cup vegetable oil
1 tablespoon poppy seeds

Combine sugar, onion salt, and mustard in electric mixer bowl. Add vinegar; blend. While mixer is running, gradually add oil. Beat for 5 minutes. Add poppy seeds. Refrigerate.

Honey Dressing for Fruit Salad

3 tablespoons red wine vinegar
2 tablespoons honey
1 tablespoon lemon juice
1/2 cup salad oil
1/2 teaspoon finely chopped onion

1/4 cup sugar
1/2 teaspoon dry mustard
1/2 teaspoon salt
1/2 teaspoon celery seed

Combine vinegar, honey, lemon juice, salad oil, and onion in blender; blend till smooth. Add balance of ingredients and blend until well mixed. Store in refrigerator.

Irene's Dressing

1 quart mayonnaise
3 cups catsup
1 12-ounce can evaporated milk
2/3 cup sugar
1/2 teaspoon salt

1/4 teaspoon pepper
1 tablespoon garlic salt
1 cup vinegar
1 4-ounce package blue cheese,
     crumbled into very small pieces

Beat all ingredients together with an electric mixer until thick and creamy. (Thanks to Irene Hayes, Alpine, Utah.)

Savory Herb Vinegars

Most craft stores carry attractive bottles with corks; prices will vary. Or the sisters could bring bottles from home. Be sure bottles have been washed.

Use approximately 1 cup fresh herbs such as thyme, sage, dill, tarragon, mint, basil, rosemary, or parsley. With a bamboo skewer, push herbs into bottle. You could also add garlic cloves, hot chili peppers, whole spices or seeds, or lemon or lime rinds cut in curls. Be sure herbs have been washed.

Fill bottle with vinegar—red wine, white wine vinegar, cider, or plain vinegar. Replace cork, or seal with wax (see page 33 of first volume of *Homemaking Blueprints* for instructions on sealing bottles with wax).

Allow vinegar to steep in a sunny window for 2–3 days. Tie on a label with a ribbon if you want to use the vinegar as a gift.

Fragrant Potpourri Doorknob Hanger

A number of scrapbook stores sell decorative printed 8½x11-inch sheets of paper; a gingham pattern is a good choice for this project. Buy one sheet of paper for each doorknob hanger. Cut 2½ inches off the 11-inch side of the paper (see illustration 1) so that the paper is 6 inches wide and 11 inches long (see illustration 2). With the 6-inch edge of the paper toward you, fold the bottom edge of the sheet up 4 inches (see illustration 3), being sure the patterned side of the paper is out. Fold the top edge down to form an envelope flap (see illustration 4). Find the middle of the top flap, finger pinch the center, and fold back sides so that you have a line on which to cut the envelope flap evenly. Cut the top flaps on angled fold lines (see illustration 5, next page) with scalloped scissors. Cut the sides of the envelope through both layers to form an attractive edge to the main body of the envelope. Adjust the tension on your sewing machine so that it will have the proper tension for paper (experiment on a plain piece of folded paper until stitch is even on both sides of paper). Sew a ¼-inch seam along each side of the envelope from the bottom of the envelope to the point where the top flap begins (see illustration 6). Fill the

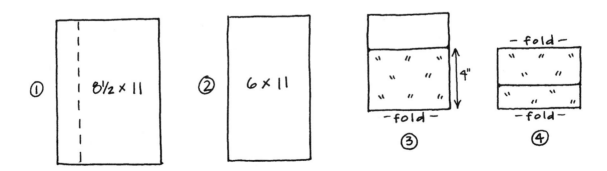

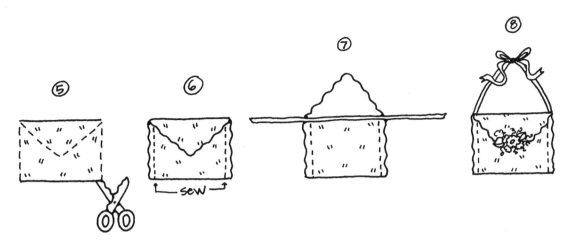

envelope with potpourri. Cut a 30-inch piece of $1/8$-inch ribbon. Lay the ribbon across top of envelope underneath the flap, and secure with tape on both ends (see illustration 7). Close flap and seal with a rolled piece of tape under the flap so that tape is not visible. Bring ends of ribbon together and tie a knot; then tie a bow with ends of ribbon. Glue dried or silk flowers to flap of envelope with white glue (see illustration 8). Allow to dry. (You could also use a pretty sticker on the flap of the envelope.)

"This Old House"

Have someone in your ward who is adept at making simple home repairs teach the class. Each sister could also make her own toolbox—one that is off-limits to husband and children. Buy a metal tackle box at the hardware store. There are rub-on decals now available at craft stores that can be adhered to the box. This attractive box will alert the family that the box is Mom's, and tools are not to be removed at any time!

Alternative Themes and Miniclasses

Theme: Sunny Side Up

Invitation: Use the sunflower pattern included here.

Miniclasses:

Sunny Delights. Share recipes using lemons, such as lemon icebox dessert (see July section for this recipe) or lemon meringue pie.

Sunny Decor. Do a sunflower craft project.

Be on the Sunny Side. Have a class on how to begin a food storage program, how to rotate your food storage, and how to store supplies in limited spaces.

A Sunny Outlook. Elder Jack H Goaslind's article in the April 1997 *Ensign* titled "Look to the Future with Optimism" (pp. 22–27) would make an excellent outline for this class.

Theme: Enjoy Bounteous Blessings . . . at Homemaking Meeting

Invitation: Type the following scripture on the invitation: "Men are, that they might have joy" (2 Nephi 2:25). Invite the sisters to count their blessings at homemaking meeting.

Miniclasses:

The Bounteous Tomato. Share recipes for preserving tomatoes—salsa, chili sauce, stewed tomatoes, etc.

Bounteous Bouquets. Give ideas for harvesting and preserving flowers from your garden.

Bounteous Words to Live By. Cross-stitch the scripture "Men are, that they might have joy" (2 Nephi 2:25).

Finding Bounteous Joy. Elder Neal A. Maxwell's talk in the April 1997 *Ensign* titled "Enduring Well" (pp. 6–10) could be used as an outline for the class.

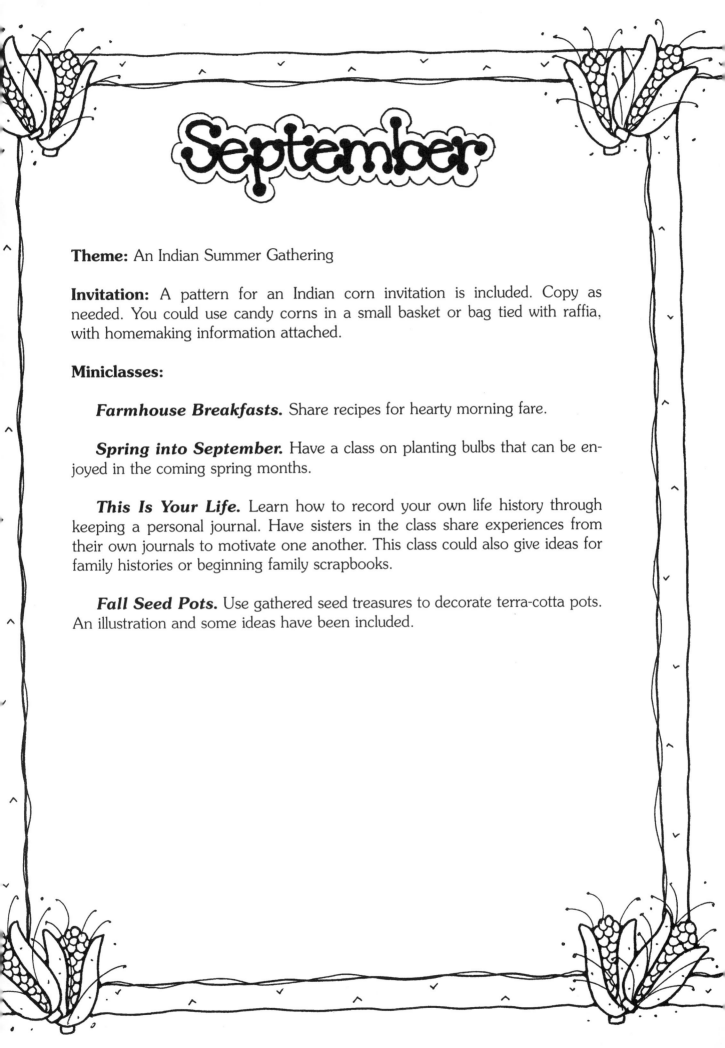

September

Theme: An Indian Summer Gathering

Invitation: A pattern for an Indian corn invitation is included. Copy as needed. You could use candy corns in a small basket or bag tied with raffia, with homemaking information attached.

Miniclasses:

Farmhouse Breakfasts. Share recipes for hearty morning fare.

Spring into September. Have a class on planting bulbs that can be enjoyed in the coming spring months.

This Is Your Life. Learn how to record your own life history through keeping a personal journal. Have sisters in the class share experiences from their own journals to motivate one another. This class could also give ideas for family histories or beginning family scrapbooks.

Fall Seed Pots. Use gathered seed treasures to decorate terra-cotta pots. An illustration and some ideas have been included.

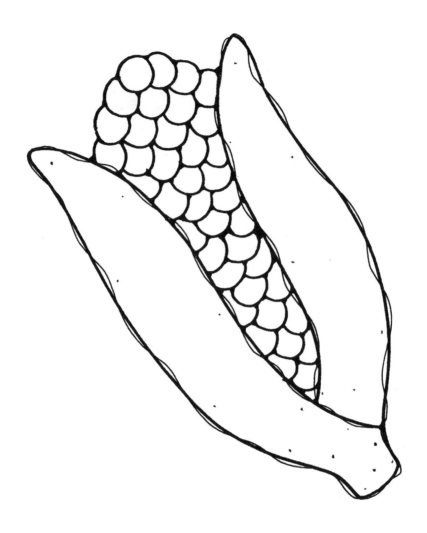

Farmhouse Breakfasts

Griddle Cakes

1 cup flour
1 teaspoon baking powder
1/2 teaspoon salt
1 tablespoon sugar

1 egg, well beaten
3/4 cup milk
3 tablespoons melted butter or shortening

   Combine flour, baking powder, salt, and sugar. Combine egg and milk. Add to flour gradually, beating to a smooth batter. Add butter or shortening. Drop griddle cake batter from tip of tablespoon onto hot, greased griddle. Bake, turning each cake when it is browned on underside and puffed and slightly set on top. Serve at once with butter and syrup or jam. Makes 12–15 griddle cakes.

Waffles

2 cups sifted cake flour
2 teaspoons baking powder
1/2 teaspoon salt
3 egg yolks, well beaten

1 cup milk
4 tablespoons melted butter
3 egg whites, stiffly beaten

Sift flour once, measure, add baking powder and salt, and sift again. Combine egg yolks and milk. Add to flour, beating until smooth. Add butter. Fold in egg whites. Bake in hot waffle iron. Makes four 4-section waffles.

Toasted Coconut Waffles. Sprinkle batter for each waffle with coconut before closing iron. Serve with syrup or butterscotch sauce.

Bacon Waffles. Sprinkle batter for each waffle with diced uncooked bacon before closing iron. Serve hot with scrambled eggs.

Diane's Bran Date Muffins

2 cups boiling water
5 teaspoons baking soda
1 cup shortening
2 cups sugar
4 eggs
1 quart buttermilk

5 cups flour
1 teaspoon salt
4 cups All-Bran or Bran Buds
2 cups bran flakes
2 cups chopped dates
1 cup walnuts

Combine boiling water and baking soda and let cool. Cream shortening and sugar together. Add eggs. Alternately add buttermilk, flour, and salt. Add baking soda and water mixture. Stir in remaining ingredients. Place in a large, well-covered container and refrigerate. Do not stir mixture after it is refrigerated. Spoon mixture into well-greased muffin tins. Bake at 375 degrees for 20 minutes. Mixture may be refrigerated for up to 3 weeks.

Fall Seed Pots

Gather colorful leaves, small pinecones, seeds, seedpods, small acorns, small dried flowers, dried berries, cattails, dried orange and apple slices, etc. Hot-glue leaves, etc., to terra-cotta pots in desired patterns. Pots can be used for plants, candles, or potpourri.

Alternative Themes and Miniclasses

Theme: A Time for Every Season!

Invitation: Include homemaking information on a cutout hourglass.

Miniclasses:

The Nurturing Years. Share helps and ideas on how to enjoy the years of young mothering and make the most of these formative years for children.

Growing Pains! Learn how to cope with the pains, trials, and joys of mothering through the teen years.

Empty Nest Years. What do we do with our lives when the children are gone from the nest? Share ideas on how to make life meaningful.

The Golden Years. Share ideas for how we can make our golden years truly golden by giving Church service, preparing for missions, genealogy work, volunteering, and so on.

Theme: An Old-Fashioned Quilting Bee

Invitation: Attach homemaking information to small quilt squares.

Have an old-fashioned quilting bee with a variety of quilts set up for the sisters to quilt or tie. These quilts could be donated to homeless shelters, women's shelters, hospitals, and so on. (Note: Animal shelters also love to receive old used quilts or small blankets!)

Conclude the quilting bee with a potluck luncheon, with each sister bringing her favorite recipe to share.

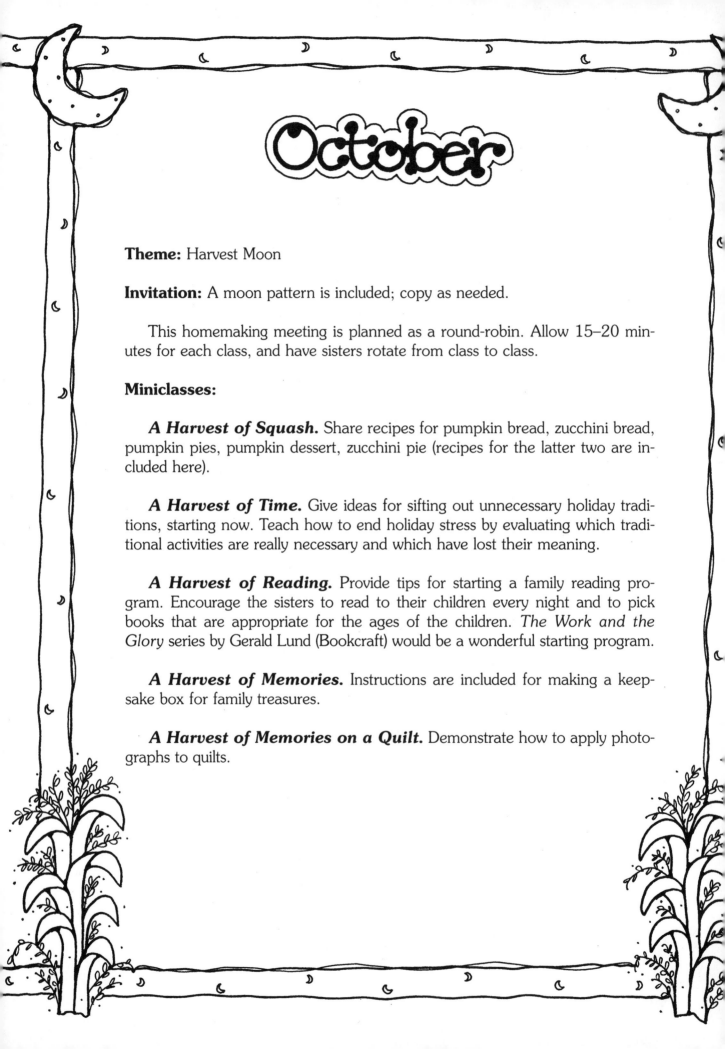

October

Theme: Harvest Moon

Invitation: A moon pattern is included; copy as needed.

This homemaking meeting is planned as a round-robin. Allow 15–20 minutes for each class, and have sisters rotate from class to class.

Miniclasses:

A Harvest of Squash. Share recipes for pumpkin bread, zucchini bread, pumpkin pies, pumpkin dessert, zucchini pie (recipes for the latter two are included here).

A Harvest of Time. Give ideas for sifting out unnecessary holiday traditions, starting now. Teach how to end holiday stress by evaluating which traditional activities are really necessary and which have lost their meaning.

A Harvest of Reading. Provide tips for starting a family reading program. Encourage the sisters to read to their children every night and to pick books that are appropriate for the ages of the children. *The Work and the Glory* series by Gerald Lund (Bookcraft) would be a wonderful starting program.

A Harvest of Memories. Instructions are included for making a keepsake box for family treasures.

A Harvest of Memories on a Quilt. Demonstrate how to apply photographs to quilts.

A Harvest of Squash

Pumpkin Dessert

Yellow cake mix
1 1/2 cups finely chopped pecans
1 cup margarine or butter, melted

Mix together:

1 29-ounce can pumpkin
1 12-ounce can evaporated milk
3 eggs

4 teaspoons pumpkin pie spice
1/2 teaspoon salt

Pour pumpkin mixture into greased 9x13x2-inch cake pan. Sprinkle half of yellow cake mix over top of pumpkin mixture—yes, dry mix! Sprinkle pecans over top of cake mix. Drizzle melted butter or margarine over top of cake mix. Bake for 1 hour at 350 degrees or until a knife inserted in center comes out clean. Serve with sweetened whipped cream or whipped topping.

Zucchini Pie

1/4 cup margarine or butter
4 cups sliced zucchini
1 cup chopped onion
1/2 cup chopped fresh parsley or
    2 tablespoons dry parsley
1/2 teaspoon salt
1/2 teaspoon pepper
1/4 teaspoon garlic powder

1/4 teaspoon basil
1/4 teaspoon oregano
2 eggs, well beaten
2 cups grated mozzarella cheese
1 package Pillsbury refrigerated
    crescent dinner rolls
2 teaspoons prepared mustard

Melt butter or margarine in saucepan; saute zucchini slices and onions for 10 minutes or just until tender. Add parsley, salt, pepper, garlic powder, basil, and oregano. Remove from heat and cool. Stir zucchini into eggs; add cheese. Let stand 10 minutes. Meanwhile, press crescent rolls into 9-inch pie plate; spread with mustard. Pour zucchini/egg mixture into pie plate. Bake 18–20 minutes at 375 degrees or until center is set.

A Harvest of Memories

A Family Keepsake Box

Materials needed:

Round wooden shaker box
Crocheted doily to fit top of box (craft stores stock inexpensive doilies)
18 inches of 2 1/2-inch-wide ribbon
Wire
Ribbon roses (assorted sizes and colors of ribbon roses can be purchased at craft
    stores)

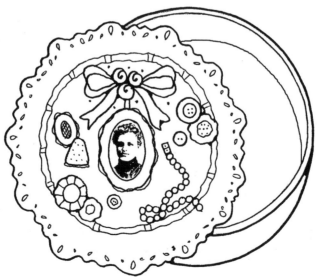

58

Sisters should also bring assorted nostalgic items from home to complete box—buttons, necklaces, gloves, jewelry pins, earrings, a locket with family picture or a very small oval frame with a picture, handkerchiefs, buttons, etc.

The box can either be used as is or painted with acrylic paints. If painted, the sisters would need to take the boxes home the month before the class and paint them, or the class leader would need to paint the boxes in advance.

Glue the doily on top of the box with white glue or a glue gun. Do not use too much glue or it will soak through the doily. Make a bow with the ribbon, wrap center with wire, and glue to upper portion of the box. Glue 3 small ribbon roses or 1 larger rose in the center of the bow. Arrange other items until you are pleased with the effect; glue in place.

A Harvest of Memories on a Quilt

There are products available at craft stores that can be used to transfer photographs onto fabric. Make a small quilt or wall hanging using a transferred photograph, and attach antique buttons, doilies, jewelry, and so on.

Alternative Themes and Miniclasses

Theme: The Pumpkin Patch

Invitation: Use a cute pumpkin shape for the invitation.

Miniclasses:

Pumpkin Goodies. Share recipes for pumpkin pie, pumpkin bread, or pumpkin desserts.

Scary Pumpkins. Carve creative jack-o'-lanterns using the new carving tools available at most novelty and craft stores.

Pumpkin Decor. Paint a pumpkin for the front door.

Don't Be like Charlie Brown, Waiting for the Great Pumpkin Who Never Comes. Give ideas for finding joy in every day. Choose a book or *Ensign* article that encourages the sisters to be optimistic and joyful about life.

Theme: A Family Country Fair

Invitation: Use a badge with ribbons, like those awarded at fairs, as the invitation. Check novelty stores for this item.

Invite the whole family to an old-fashioned family fair. Have booth games for the children and teenagers. You could have a lip-sync show or hire a caller and have square dancing. Serve snow cones, hot scones with butter and honey, and candied apples.

Theme: Holiday Beginnings

Invitation: Use the peppermint candy invitation included in the book. You could also make a cute invitation by using the heart pattern in the January section of this book. Cut out a heart from red gingham paper (available at scrapbook supply stores). Tie a cinnamon stick with a piece of raffia and glue onto the heart.

Miniclasses:

Sweet Confections. Homemade candy recipes are included.

Around the Kitchen Table. Encourage sisters to have the family all gather for dinner each evening. See Elder LeGrand R. Curtis' talk "A Table Encircled with Love," *Ensign,* May 1995, pages 82–83. Suggest that the sisters read a Christmas story each night after dinner during the Christmas season.

Stretch Beyond Your Own Neighborhood. Encourage sisters to find ways for their families to help others in the community who are in need. Often the local newspaper has names of families who need help. Make this a family or ward activity.

Advent Memories. A pattern for an advent calendar is included.

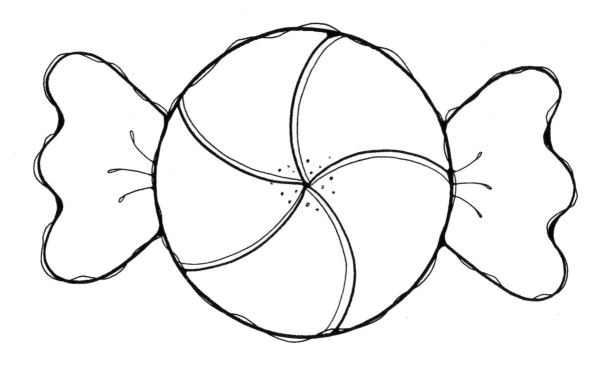

Sweet Confections

Old-Fashioned Fudge

2 cups sugar
2 tablespoons powdered cocoa
3/4 cup milk or light cream

2 tablespoons butter
1 teaspoon vanilla
1 cup chopped pecans

Combine sugar and cocoa; add milk. Over medium heat, stir until sugar is completely dissolved. After sugar is dissolved, do not stir again until candy is cooked, or the fudge will be grainy. Allow to cook until candy reaches 234 degrees on a candy thermometer (be sure the bulb of candy thermometer does not rest on bottom of saucepan) or until syrup dropped into very cold water forms a soft ball which flattens when removed from water. Remove from heat. Add butter and vanilla. Do not stir. Cool until lukewarm. Beat with wooden spoon until fudge loses gloss (fudge will hold its shape). Add nuts before fudge gets too thick. Quickly spread into buttered 8x8x2-inch pan. Cool. Cut into squares.

Divinity

3 cups sugar

1/2 cup water

1/2 cup white light corn syrup

2 egg whites

1/2 teaspoon vanilla

1/2 cup chopped pecans

Over medium heat, stir sugar, water, and syrup together until sugar is dissolved. Cook, without stirring, until syrup forms a soft ball when dropped in very cold water or until it reaches 234 degrees on candy thermometer. While cooking syrup, beat egg whites until they form soft peaks. After syrup is cooked, remove from heat, and while still hot, gradually pour syrup over egg whites while mixer is running. Do not scrape the syrup from the pan, or candy will become grainy. Just continue pouring until all syrup that will drip from pan is added to egg whites. Continue beating until mixture is a very thick consistency. Add vanilla and nuts and drop from spoon onto cookie sheets which have been lined with waxed paper. Allow to cool until thoroughly set; store in airtight container.

Around the Kitchen Table

The article "A Table Encircled with Love" by Elder LeGrand R. Curtis (*Ensign,* May 1995, pp. 82–83) could be used for your class. There are also a number of books on the market with wonderful collections of short Christmas stories that could be read each night at the dinner table. One excellent book is *Twelve Tales of Christmas* by Richard Siddoway (Salt Lake City: Bookcraft, 1992).

Advent Memories

Christmas Advent Calendar

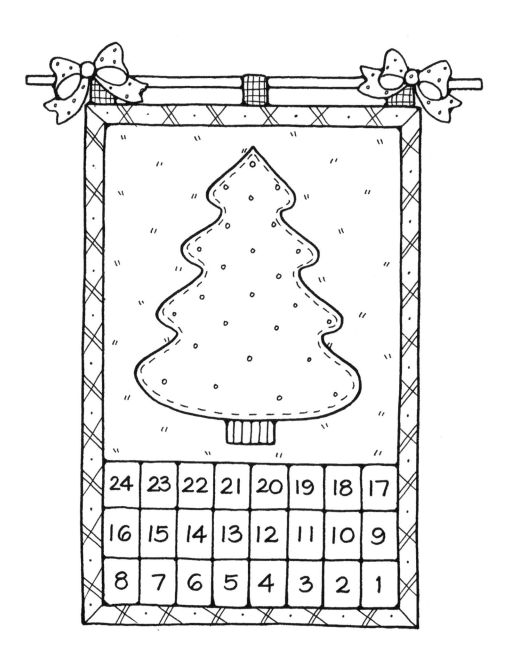

We have had advent calendars similar to this in our homes for 25 years. The calendar was originally designed in felt by Joylyn Cluny of Salt Lake City, and she gave one to each of our families as Christmas gifts. She made patterns for the tree ornaments from greeting cards. We have adapted her design using modern quilting techniques, and Annette Ward has designed a darling set of nativity figures. We hope you will enjoy this project. Thanks to Joylyn for the original idea!

This is a rather complicated project for a miniclass, but with advanced preparation, the sisters can finish the project during the meeting. Although this is a more expensive and complicated project than others we have included in the book, the calendar will become a cherished Christmas tradition. Draw each pattern on poster board using the dimensions given in diagram 1, and cut the fabrics according to the patterns. This advance preparation will also save money since the patterns could be manipulated to save fabric. Make several copies of the number patterns (see page 68) on cover-weight paper stock, and cut them out so the sisters can trace their patterns during the meeting.

Copy several sets of the patterns for the nativity figures so the sisters can trace the figures onto the shrink-art plastic. They can take the plastic sheets home and let their children color the figures for a family night activity. Children love to watch the plastic shrink in the oven.

First, and most important, read the instructions carefully before beginning the project!

Materials needed:

1 1/4 yards (45 inches) red fabric (small overall print, gingham, or small plaid—predominant color should be red) for banner
2/3 yard (45 inches) fabric (contrasting print—predominant color should be green) for binding, tabs, bows, and numbers
2x1 1/2-inch piece of brown fabric for tree trunk
1/2 yard plush felt (green to match fabrics) for tree
1/2 yard lightweight batting
12 yards linen thread (very fine twine)
24 6mm double ring gold jewelry rings (available at craft or jewelry-making stores)
8 inches fusible binding
4 sheets shrink-art plastic (8 1/2x11 inches)
Permanent pens or colored pencils (see instructions for shrink plastic)
1/2 inch dowel—21 inches long

Cutting instructions:

Cut 2 pieces of red fabric, 17x24 inches, for the banner.
Cut 3 pieces of red fabric, 5x17 inches, for pockets. (These pieces should be cut on the grain of the fabric or the pockets will sag. See diagram 1.)
Cut 2 pieces of green fabric, 2x25 inches, for side bindings.
Cut 2 pieces of green fabric, 2x18 inches, for top and bottom bindings.
Note: If you want to use a bias binding, you will need to buy more fabric so you can cut it into long strips on the bias. However, it is not necessary to have a bias binding on straight edges.
Cut 3 pieces of green fabric, 6x5 inches, for tabs.
Tear or cut 2 strips of green fabric, 30x2 inches, for bows on ends of dowel.
Enlarge tree pattern on page 69 to 14 inches high. Cut tree out of plush felt.
Cut trunk of tree, 2x1 1/2 inches, from brown fabric.
Cut a 14x5-inch piece of green fabric for the numbers on the pockets.

Assembly:

Fold (5x17) pocket strips in half with the right sides out so they measure 17x1$\frac{1}{2}$ inches. Press the folded edge. Place raw edges of bottom pocket strip on bottom edge of the banner front, right sides of material facing you; pin in place. Place middle pocket strip with the cut edges $\frac{1}{4}$ inch under folded edge of bottom pocket; pin in place. Place top pocket strip with cut edges $\frac{1}{4}$ inch under folded edge of middle pocket; pin in place. Sew pocket strips $\frac{1}{8}$ inch in from raw edges. (See diagram 2.) Lay banner on table and measure $\frac{1}{2}$ inch in from each side edge of banner; mark at top and bottom of each side, and draw a line down sides of banner with a disappearing marking pencil or chalk. Lay ruler along top edge of top pocket strip and mark every 2 inches across the strip, starting from line on side of banner. Repeat on bottom edge of banner. Draw a chalk line from the bottom mark to the top mark to make a line on which to sew pockets. Sew along chalked lines to form pockets. (See diagram 3.) Sew $\frac{1}{2}$ inch in along sides of banner to secure pockets to banner. You should now have 8 2-inch pockets across the banner on each of the 3 rows of pockets, which creates a total of 24 pockets.

Fuse a 2x1$\frac{1}{2}$-inch piece of brown fabric to fusible bonding. Place tree on banner as shown in completed illustration, and position trunk under bottom of tree. Pin trunk in place. Remove tree and adhere trunk to banner. Pin tree in place. Using the linen thread, sew tree onto banner with a running stitch or blanket stitch. (Note: Plush felt is too heavy to adhere with fusible bonding, and the plush look is crushed by a hot iron.) Position 24 gold rings on tree, spacing evenly so they cover tree; pin in place. Stitch rings onto tree with green thread.

Lay the fabric cut for the back of banner right side down, with the wrong side facing you. Lay batting on top of backing. Place completed top of banner on batting, face up. Pin layers together. Pin binding to edges of banner through all layers of fabric and batting. Sew $\frac{1}{2}$-inch seam along edge of banner, and trim seam edge to $\frac{1}{4}$ inch. Fold binding to back of banner, turn under $\frac{1}{4}$ inch, and slip stitch to back of banner. Repeat with bindings on top and bottom of banner. Miter corners.

Adhere 5x14-inch piece of green fabric to bonding material. On paper side of bonding, trace numbers. (See patterns and number of each numeral needed.) Be sure to trace number patterns backwards since you are tracing on the wrong side of the fabric—when numbers are adhered to pockets, they will be in the wrong direction if you don't trace them backwards. Cut out numbers, remove paper backing, and adhere to pockets on banner, starting with 24 on the first pocket as shown in completed illustration.

Fold the 3 6x5-inch tabs in half so they measure 6x2$\frac{1}{2}$ inches. Sew $\frac{1}{4}$-inch seam down the 6-inch raw edges; turn and press. Attach tabs to banner as shown in finished illustration by machine or hand stitching. Run the dowel through the tabs, and tie 30x2-inch torn strips into bows on outer edges of tabs (see finished illustration).

Shrink-art plastic tree ornaments:

Trace the patterns for the nativity figures onto clear shrink-art plastic with a fine permanent pen. Color the figures with colored permanent pens or colored pencils. We discovered quite by accident that certain brands of colored pencils will work on shrink plastic. The brands we found that worked well were Dixon Custom Color, Design Spectrocolor by Faber-Castel, and Berol Prismacolor; other brands would not work at all. The colored pencils create softer colors and are easier and less messy for children to use than permanent markers. If you do use permanent markers, color lightly because the colors will be much deeper when the plastic shrinks. Pilot brand gold and silver markers make wonderful accents on your designs.

Cut out figures. Punch a hole in the top of each figure with at least a 1/4-inch punch. Heat oven to 275 degrees. Place several figures on a cookie sheet, but do not allow them to touch. Shrinkage time will vary. The first batch of figures will take longer to shrink because the cookie sheet needs to heat. It may take as long as 5 or 6 minutes for the cookie sheet to heat and the figure to shrink to desired size. When the cookie sheet is hot, the figures may shrink to desired size in 2–3 minutes. Each figure will curl up and shrink down to approximately 1 1/2 inches. Be sure to let the figures shrink completely or they will not fit in the pockets on the banner.

If you do not have a window in your oven so that you can watch the shrinking process, check the figures every 2 or 3 minutes. If they curl up and do not uncurl, you can flatten them with a spatula or pancake turner. Press firmly with the pancake turner to flatten. They may stick to the cookie sheet but can be loosened with the spatula and then pressed flat on the hot cookie sheet. (Caution: Do not remove from oven and allow to cool, or you cannot straighten them out.) Check at your craft store for specific instructions for the brand of shrink-art plastic they carry.

Thread 8-inch pieces of linen thread through figures, tie a knot at top of each figure so it does not slip off, and place in pockets of the banner.

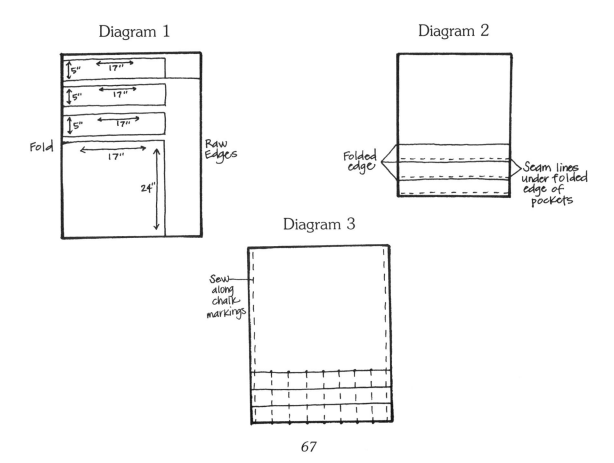

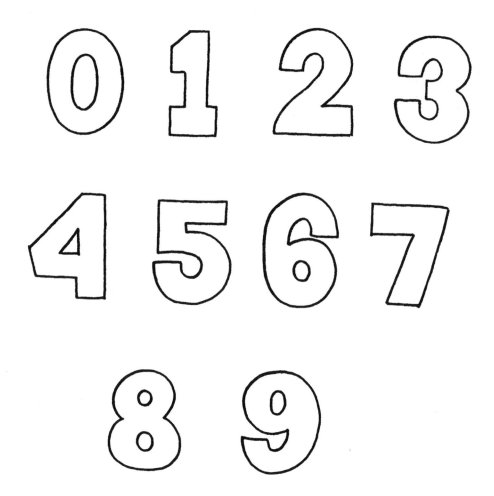

Cut 13 of the number 1.
Cut 8 of the number 2.
Cut 3 of the number 3.
Cut 3 of the number 4.
Cut 2 of the number 5.
Cut 2 of the number 6.
Cut 2 of the number 7.
Cut 2 of the number 8.
Cut 2 of the number 9.
Cut 2 of the number 0.

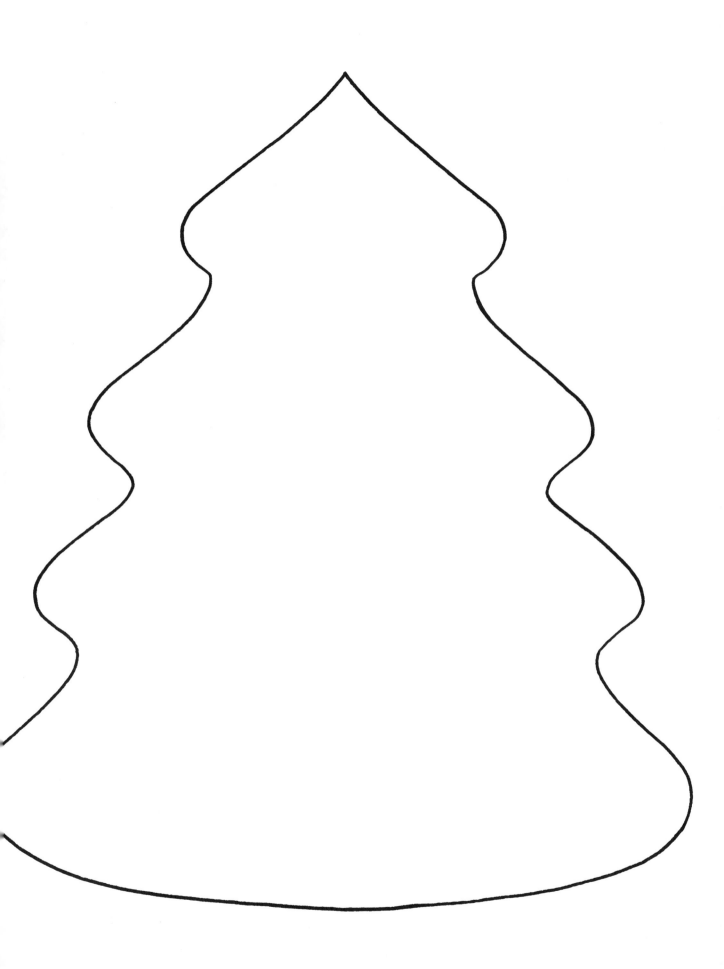

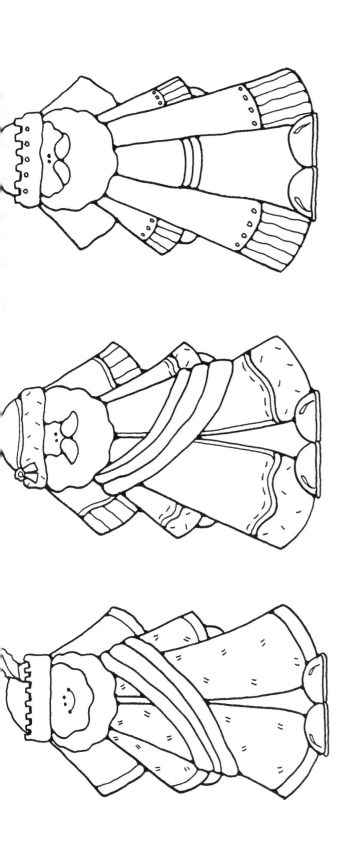

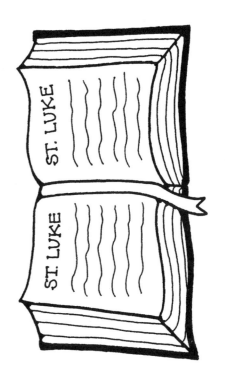

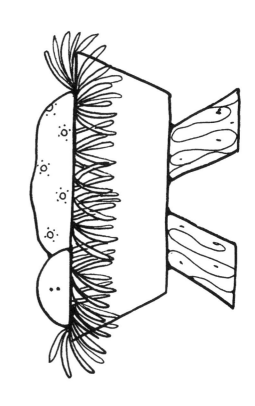

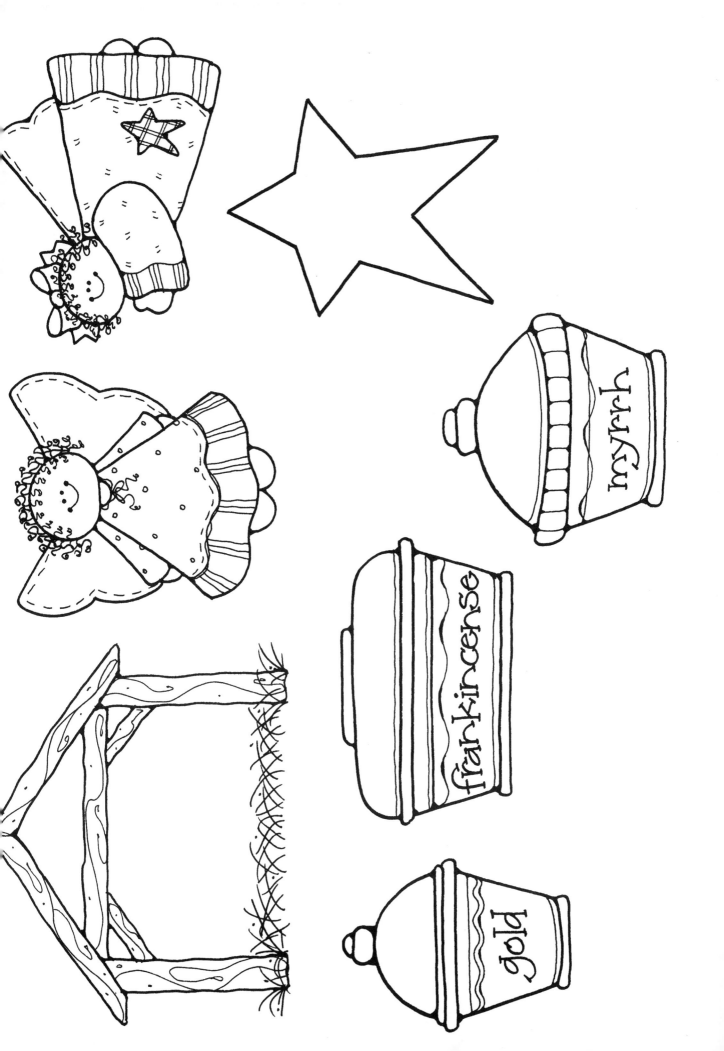

Alternative Themes and Miniclasses

Theme: Count Your Blessings

Invitation: Cut out a block *B* (about 4 inches high) and write the message on the letter. Scatter numbers all around your message.

Miniclasses:

The Blessings of Good Nutrition. Teach the importance of serving balanced meals, especially during the holiday season when so many treats are available.

Blessings of the Past. Have sisters share ideas for teaching children about their ancestors.

Count Your Blessings. Do a simple cross-stitch bookmark or wall hanging that says "Count Your Blessings." Find a pattern at the stitchery store, or chart your own simple pattern.

Recognizing Your Blessings. Have an optimistic sister who has successfully faced many challenges tell how she has dealt with her difficulties. Stress the positive.

Theme: Holiday Hustle and Bustle: Help at Homemaking Meeting for Combating Holiday Stress

Invitation: Attach your message to an evergreen sprig with bright red ribbon.

Miniclasses:

No-Stress Cooking. Save time during the holidays by cooking Crock-Pot meals.

Gifts from the Heart. Give ideas for service coupons or gifts of time spent helping others as alternatives to spending money on Christmas gifts.

No-Hassle Door Wreaths. Make a simple last-minute wreath using the live wreaths available at Christmas tree lots. Show how to use a showy bow and a few pinecones to make a simple, fast wreath. If wreaths are too expensive, buy a few boughs, wire together, and attach a bow and pinecones to boughs.

A Quiet Moment. Review books that deal with the real meaning of the holiday season, to be read in quiet moments.

Theme: Jingle All the Way!

Invitation: A pattern for a bell has been included. You could also use a real bell and attach homemaking information with a red ribbon.

Miniclasses:

December is a good month to have a round-robin format so everyone has the opportunity to attend each class.

Lollipop, Lollipop! Learn how to make your own lollipops for Christmas to give as gifts. Directions are included for making "Oreo" lollipops.

Sharing Christmas Stories. This is a wonderful month to read to your children or to read as a family. Read a different Christmas story or legend each night. Have each sister share her favorite Christmas story or book. Begin a family tradition of purchasing a new Christmas book each year and reading the book together as a family on Christmas Eve. Don't forget to read the most important Christmas story of all—the birth of our Savior!

Neighbor Gifts. Share ideas for easy and meaningful gifts to give to neighbors and friends. A recipe and idea for cinnamon potpourri bags is included.

Christmas Candles. Directions are included for making herb, flower, or Christmas motif candles to give as gifts.

Mr. Snowman. Share ideas for decorating, making, and giving snowmen. Ideas for real snowmen would be fun for those lucky enough to live where there is snow!

Lollipop, Lollipop

Oreo Lollipops

DoubleStuf Oreo cookies
Lollipop sticks
3 ounces molding chocolate

2 teaspoons vegetable oil
3 ounces white chocolate
Chopped nuts, sprinkles, etc.

Open up the DoubleStuf Oreos (those with double the frosting in the middle). Remove a tiny slit of the frosting on the outside edge of the cookie. Insert a lollipop stick into the slit, pushing the stick into the frosting. Replace the top of the cookie. You now have a lollipop ready to dip in chocolate. Melt the chocolate with 1 teaspoon vegetable oil in the microwave at 100% power for 1 minute; stir until smooth. Prepare the white chocolate in the same manner. Dip the Oreos in the chocolate and then in chopped nuts, sprinkles, etc., or drizzle with leftover chocolate, using white on the dark chocolate and dark on the white chocolate. Place on waxed paper on cookie sheets and chill until chocolate is hardened.

Neighbor Gifts

Potpourri Bags

4 ounces cinnamon sticks, broken in
    small pieces
2 ounces minced orange peel
1/2 ounce crushed nutmeg
12 drops each of cinnamon, allspice,
    and orange oil
1 ounce whole cloves
3 ounces whole allspice
1/2 ounce ginger

Combine spices and oils and place in a covered container. Allow to set for about 3 weeks. Make small bags using Christmas fabric. Fill the bags with the potpourri and tie with raffia or a ribbon, attaching greenery, cinnamon sticks, or other desired items.

Christmas Candles

Gather leaves, flower petals, fresh bay leaves or other herbs, ferns, berries, and so on. Use a large-size white or ivory candle. Using a heat-proof container taller and wider than the candle (a tin can works well), fill the container with enough hot water to reach the top of the candle when it is immersed. Holding the candle by the wick, immerse it in the hot water for about 30 seconds. Remove the candle and press the flowers, herbs, etc., onto the softened wax. Refill the container with more very hot water and dip the candle again briefly to seal the herbs or flowers. Remove from the water and cool.

Alternative Themes and Miniclasses

Theme: Home for the Holidays

Invitation: Make a small map of the homes to be visited and attach instructions for a Christmas home tour.

This is such a busy month and a fun time for parties and visiting. Instead of having classes, plan a homemaking Christmas home tour. Make plans ahead of time with sisters who would be willing to open their homes to share their holiday decor and ideas. The number of homes would depend on the number of sisters participating and the distance needing to be traveled in your area. If you have a large group of sisters, divide into groups, visiting different homes at a time. Have all sisters or groups meet together at the last home on the tour, allowing time for refreshments and visiting. If funds allow, make a small remembrance for each sister as a gift from the Relief Society presidency.

Theme: Welcome Home

Invitation: A pattern for a house can be found in *Homemaking Blueprints,* volume 1, page 59. A small candle with homemaking information attached with a ribbon could also be used.

Miniclasses:

Christmas Wassail. Share recipes for making wassail. Send each sister home with a small bag of wassail mix.

Helping Hands at Christmas. Discuss the opportunities in your area to give service by helping at food service banks. Have each sister bring a can of food to homemaking and put together a box of Christmas goodies to donate to the needy.

Welcome the Spirit of Christmas into Your Home. Share ideas for bringing the true spirit of Christmas into your home. Teach ways to help children catch the spirit of giving to others.

Light-the-Way Candles. Using beeswax sheets, wrap candles. Three candles wrapped together with ribbons and greenery make a great Christmas decoration.

Sign-up Sheet